TOURING CAR YEAR 95-96

The official review of the Auto Trader RAC British Touring Car Championship 1995

First Published 1995

Haymarket Specialist Motoring Publications Ltd

ISBN 0-86024-925-5

Typesetting by OTS Typesetting Ltd, Caterham
Printing by BR Hubbard, Chesterfield
Binding by Butler & Tanner, Frome
Distribution by Vine House Distribution
Design by Francis Jago, MPA Fingal and Autosport Special Projects

Publisher Martin Nott

Haymarket Specialist Motoring Publications Ltd
38-42 Hampton Road
Teddington
Middlesex   TW11 0JE
Tel: 0181-943 5000
Fax: 0181-943 5850

The Auto Trader RAC
British Touring Car Championship is organised by:
TOCA Ltd
The Manor, Haseley Business Park, Warwick CV35 7LS
Tel: 01203 537037 Fax: 01203 537038

Contents

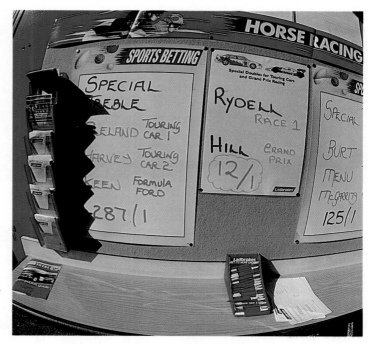

PHOTOGRAPHY: AUTOSPORT, BOTHWELL, RALPH HARDWICK, HAGGATY

Welcome to the best of 1995

The Auto Trader RAC British Touring Car Championship

just keeps getting bigger and better, doesn't it?

Alan Gow, managing director of TOCA Limited explains.

4

1995 saw a tremendous battle for the drivers, Total Cup and manufacturers championships. This annual book pays tribute to those winners as they all thoroughly deserve their success. I also want to make special mention to everyone else that maybe did not achieve the results they had hoped for. Just to compete in, and against the best in the world is something that most drivers or teams aspire to, but few achieve. Every one of them should take great pride in the fact that they were beaten only by the very best in the world of touring car racing.

And that is what our championship is, the best Super Touring Car Championship in the world and by any measure - crowd figures, TV audiences, manufacturer involvement, the quality of the teams and the drivers, and the competitiveness of the racing.

To underline this I'm very proud that the official world-wide TV audience figures have shown that in 1995 just over 1 billion people watched this series. Just think about the figure for a moment: over one billion viewers, in more than 100 countries around the world watched over 62,000 minutes of the BTCC on TV.

Who'd have though it possible only a few years ago? We now rank with the very top in global motorsport TV coverage. This is not just a domestic British Championship, this is a championship that is both internationally recognised and viewed by literally many million … as the very best.

With our 1996 plans in place, next year will certainly see further increases in our exposure. 1996 also sees the introduction of Super Touring into

North America, an important milestone in insuring the long-term success of this racing. Whilst TOCA are now involved in three major championships in three different continents, our commitment to the BTCC is very much undiminished and unfilled.

The BTCC will remain as the cornerstone of Super Touring racing and the core of TOCA's business … nothing will be allowed to detract from our efforts right here.

We are not involved in other championships just for our own sake. It's in all our interests to ensure that Super Touring is firmly established at the forefront of international motorsport, in as many markets as possible, for the long-term good. It's a cunning plan … and despite what some other people may wish to happen … I think it might just work!

Thanks again for a great season and to use a quaint Australian phrase … I look forward to seeing your backside trackside in 1996.

Powering ahead.

Auto Trader is again the prime sponsor of the RAC British Touring Car Championship. Published in 13 regional editions each packed with pictures of thousands of cars, there's no better way of bringing buyers and sellers together. That's why Britain's best selling motoring magazine attracts nearly 2 million* readers every week.

Auto Trader

Britain's favourite motoring weekly.

(*1.967M NRS Jan-Dec 1994.)

Welcome from Auto Trader

PHOTOGRAPHY: RALPH HARDWICK, SUTTON, JACKIE DANE

We are at the end of another great season of racing in the Auto Trader RAC British Touring Car Championship. Once again Britain's premier motor racing series has lived up to everyone's expectations, with close action, not only at the front of the field, but also amongst the privateer Total Cup runners.

The Auto Trader RAC British Touring Car Championship has continued to attract top line drivers from Formula One, and the best young stars from the Total Cup. This year we even have a home champion to cheer. The crowds have continued to flock to the circuits in even greater numbers, and they have been rewarded with more races. The 1995 championship consisted of 25 rounds, two at each meeting, with the only exception being the British Grand Prix. Next year this will also have two rounds, one on Saturday and one on Sunday. The world-wide TV viewing figures continue to grow, with many millions following the fortunes of the drivers, who many of you are able to meet at the races.

Auto Trader would like to thank all the competitors in the championship for their efforts, however big or small, and all the organisers and clubs for their continued efforts. We must also thank all the competitors in all of the support races, which make up a big part of the entertainment for the public.

Auto Trader has been the title sponsor of the British Touring Car Championship for three years, having been involved prior to that in one way or another for several years. This sponsorship has been of great benefit to Auto Trader, and has helped us to continue to be Britain's biggest circulation motoring magazine.

We are very pleased that the Auto Trader Touring Car Championship sponsorship is continuing for at least another two years, making us one of the longest serving sponsors of this great series.

Auto Trader hopes that you will enjoy reading about the 1995 Championship, and we look forward to an even more exciting and successful 1996.

The Top Six

Touring Car Year has again asked four top motor racing journalists to pick their personal top six driver from the 1995 BTCC

LAURENCE FOSTER
AUTOSPORT

ALAIN MENU

The Swiss star is now almost unarguably the most complete Super Touring driver in the world. At the end of the season, he was simply untouchable. Early season teething trouble blunted his title challenge, but his performances at Donington's season-opener, when the paint was barely dry on the first Williams-build Renault Laguna, set the tone for a brilliant season.

JOHN CLELAND

A vintage year, when the Scot finally had all the factors to his liking and proceeded to make the most of it all.

RICKARD RYDELL

In the early part of the season, you wouldn't have taken bets against the Swede becoming the third overseas BTCC champ in a row. But as the rest improved, Volvo lost some of their early season form.

JULIAN BAILEY

For the second year running, the results will again show no podium for the former Formula 1 driver. But Bailey's speed and skill in a 2-litre touring car remain unquestioned. Bailey is still a potential BTCC champion – as ever all he needs now is the equipment to do the job.

KELVIN BURT

when Ford's struggles turned to almost despair in the second half of the season, it was Burt who responded the best.

PAUL RADISICH

Slipped from fourth to sixth in my rankings from last year. Still an ace when the circumstances allow.

JONATHAN GILL
AUTO EXPRESS

JOHN CLELAND

Perhaps not the fastest but certainly the most consistent of the 1995 front-runners … and, as all 25 rounds score, that's decisive. So John owes this top ranking here to the boys at Ray Mallock Engineering for their faultless preparation. A true team victory.

ALAIN MENU

Ultimately Menu is probably the best of the current bunch. Top qualifier, most race wins, most laps led, most fastest laps … but title bid scuppered by a couple of silly mechanical gremlins. Must start as 1996 favourite … like Paul Radisich did in '95.

JAMES THOMPSON

Raw, aggressive, spectacular and fast … that's our James. His arrival at Vauxhall forced Cleland to up his game and hence win the crown. It can be no coincidence that Vauxhall's run of victories virtually dried up after his horrific accident at

RICKARD RYDELL

Thirteen poles, four wins … need I say more. With better starts Rickard would have been champion – that's his only Achilles Heel – but in a series as competitive as the BTCC you can ill afford to throw away qualifying advantages.

WILL HOY

Despite being out qualified, out raced and out 'lucked' by team-mate Menu for the first half of the season, Will never lost heart or self belief. It was his late charge which ultimately won Renault the Manufacturers' honours.

KELVIN BURT

Bailey, Brabham, Harvey, Leslie, Radisich, Watts … I could make a case for any one of them; but my final top six spot goes to Kelvin Burt for beating his illustrious team-mate in every race after mid-June, World Cup included.

MARK FOGARTY
AUSTRALIAN AUTO ACTION

ALAIN MENU

The most complete driver. Fast, fearless

stated acumen. No obvious or exploitable weaknesses. End-of-season supremacy and top score of seven wins indicate that if Williams hadn't been wobbly on consistency, the savvy Swiss would've claimed the crown.

JOHN CLELAND
Played the percentages perfectly. The canny Caledonian tempered his ruthless racer instinct, capitalising on the Cavalier's snazzy chassis and bullet-proof reliability. Speed and tenacity complemented by title-clinching consistency. Wicked wit will ensure his reign will be notable and quotable.

RICKARD RYDELL
Fast but flawed, Record 13 pole positions undermined by slovenly starts and enigmatic errors. Had the pace and grace to be champion, but couldn't maintain early momentum. Regarded by rivals as suspect under pressure, especially self-induced. Needs more commitment and composure to realise his potential.

JAMES THOMPSON
Kick-ass kid proved you don't have to be grey to be good. Kamikaze qualifier and

ruthless racer with a complete disregard for reputations. Before sidelined by Knockhill test tumble, performance characterised by scintillating speed and elementary errors. Prodigious potential.

WILL HOY
Wily ex-champ displayed grit and resilience, battling through mid-season confidence crisis. Floundered in the first half-season, frustrated form after team administered a little TLC and got rid of the gremlins. Late podium plunder, including three cleverly crafted wins, restored his reputation and saved his seat.

KELVIN BURT
Heart belongs to single-seaters, but used his head to adapt in tin tops and make the most of a recalcitrant car. Rarely a match for Mondeomeister Paul Radisich in qualifying, the former British F3 champion's racecraft and smooth, effortless speed earned increasing accolades. If isn't lost to F1 aspirations, a future force with a top team.

NICK PHILLIPS
AUTOCAR

JOHN CLELAND
A near-perfect year for the veteran. And typically when he did get it wrong (only at round three and four at Brands), he did it on a grand scale. Consistent point-scoring – and his ability to make up two or three places when not on the front two rows, was a crucial element – won him the title.

ALAIN MENU
Super-quick, very cool, and almost impossible to pass when he's in a position of strength. A bit more car reliability in the early season would have made him champion. His time will come.

RICKARD RYDELL
Blistering quick and fast developing into a superb all-rounder. His superiority over Tim Harvey was more marked than Menu's in '94. Still occasional weaknesses in his armoury – early season starting and the ability to overcome poor grid placings late season – but he's improving fast.

WILL HOY
Weak early season, but showed all his old skill over last eight rounds. When it's going right he's one of the drivers who can deliver and he's still one of the better BTCC overtakers.

JAMES THOMPSON
Brilliant new talent. Matched or bettered Cleland for speed and was rapidly developing his racing skills before being sidelined by his testing accident. Those that took his place showed that living with Cleland was no easy task.

KELVIN BURT
Difficult season in the off-form Mondeo. But, once he'd got some mileage under his belt, whenever an opportunity to shine arose (usually on wet tracks) he did - out-driving a high-quality driver (Paul Radisich) over the second half of the season.

The People's Champion

Most sporting champions have different public and private faces,

but John Cleland race driver and John Cleland car dealer

are one and the same

GRAPHICS: JIM BAMBER

John Cleland has now won the British Touring Car Championship twice. The first time he did it was back in 1989, when he dominated his class against very little opposition. Then it raised no comment that a part-timer had won, that was the norm. Now in the highly professional, super-competitive world of the 1995 Auto Trader BTCC, victory by a 43- year-old Scot with four children, an aversion to physical fitness, who runs a couple of car dealerships, is a real achievement.

Cleland has been a consistent front-runner every year since his '89 victory, but this year everything went just that little bit better and the prized title was his and he's very happy about it. 'The BTCC is by far the best championship to win - it's the best in the world.'

The signs were there, right from the start of the year. 'When I first drove the 1995 Cavalier,' says Cleland. 'I thought: `Jesus this thing is good.'' The car and the team of course played major roles in Cleland's success. It was the second year that Ray Mallock Ltd had run the full works Vauxhall programme and RML built on the excellent start made in 1994.

Cleland explains: 'Ray (Mallock) has produced a team of people and an organisation which is up with the best

of them now. The Cavalier has certainly been a major factor, but you could say that the Volvos and the Renaults should have been too. They're what I'd call second generation touring cars - our next year's Vectra will be a second or maybe even third generation car - but they've tripped themselves up with silly little things.'

Reliability of both car and driver was one area where Cleland and Vauxhall tripped up less often than the rest - Cleland was out of the points only three times, twice when he lodged in the Paddock gravel trap at Brands and once when he and the other front-runners chose the wrong tyres for the damp conditions at Snetterton. None of his title rivals could match that consistency. 'I said at the beginning of the year that six race victories would win the championship, but that you would have to be reliably up there picking up points when you weren't winning - and that is where the strength of our car/driver combination has been.'

His relationship with engineer Phil Barker is something else that Cleland cites as crucial. 'We speak the same language and he's done a great job. If you have a really good engineer that makes all the difference. I'm a driver. I'm paid to drive, not to think about technicali-

ties. I'm paid to come in and tell the engineers what it's doing and they are paid to put it right. That's what they've done and it's worked very well.'

Tyres always play a major part and Cleland is full of praise for Michelin, which Vauxhall switched to for '95. 'Michelin has been a tremendous asset,' he says. 'As far as I'm concerned, it is by far the most professional company I've ever worked with in motorsport - not just tyre company, but any company.'

Personally Cleland also feels that this year he was in better shape than ever before. That doesn't mean he'd been down the gym all winter though: 'I do not and never have believed that you have to be a 21- year-old single-seater driver, that gets up, has three Weetabix, runs triathlons and only drinks orange juice, in order to win races,' he says. 'I'm certainly not advocating two bottles of wine and a curry the night before a race, but I just don't follow the super-fit mentality. You've undoubtedly got to be fit in single-seaters, but touring cars are different. Ninety per cent of the strength is in the head and I think I've got more strength in that department than most.'

10

However he has made adjustments to his way of life this year, which he thinks have made contributions to his driving. He's hired a general manager for his Volvo and Mazda dealerships in Galashiels and spends far less time on the business than he did, on average three days a week now. `Whereas in previous years, I've tried to do too many things and not done any of them 100%. Now I'm doing this (the BTCC) 100%.'

Giving up driving to and from the circuits as he used to, clocking up 50,000 to 60,000 miles a year as he slogged down from Scotland, has been another good move. `Now I just go to the airport get on a plane and hire a little thing at the other end. I'm a lot less stressed out, so that's probably one of the secrets as well this year.'

None of this means that he thinks being a full-time professional is the best way to do his job: `I at least have a day job I can go back to, which is something that a lot of these other guys don't have and that maybe at least relieves some of the pressure.'

There's no doubt that Cleland is at his peak right now, but how many more years does he think he's got as a top-line touring car star? `I don't see myself retiring for a lot of years to come. You've got drivers like Keke Rosberg and Klaus Ludwig who are close on 50 and Peter Brock in Australia who is 50. These are some of the best touring car drivers in the world, so on that basis I've got another seven years. I'll go on as long as I enjoy it. But the moment I stop enjoying it, I'll stop, because I have something else that I can go and do. It'll probably coincide with my sons, who are karting now, starting to race properly. I'd love to race one or both of my sons. I've always envied Jimmy McRae being able to go rallying with his two son. that to me would be great.'

Gambling is fashionable in BTCC circles at the moment and right now I reckon a small punt on J Cleland winning at least one BTCC race in the year 2000 would make a lot of sense. There are certainly plenty more race wins up the Cleland sleeve.

Total Racing

The Total Cup has quickly established itself as a showcase for Privateers. In its second year it was won, convincingly, by Matt Neal - and showed that the series' underdogs can still beat the works stars

When the winner of the 1994 Total Cup said he wouldn't enter the competition again in 1995, we knew instantly that it was a success. James Kaye had used the Total Cup as a stepping stone, and now he was moving on, looking only briefly over his shoulder at the Privateers he left behind, as he joined the works ranks with Honda.

With James Thompson also moving up in 1995, as new team mate to John Cleland at Vauxhall, there was reassuring confirmation that the Total Cup really does enable Privateers to display their talents in front of the works teams they'd so dearly love to join. Although Thompson placed only fourth in the 1994 Total Cup points standings, he had successfully drawn attention to his outright speed.

There were Doubting Thomases, of course. There were those who whispered, before the 1995 season opened, that 20-year-old Thompson would destroy his tyres by mid-race, that he would destroy his cars through youthful exuberance, that he had been recruited to the Vauxhall team only because of his father's connections.

When young James took a second place in round four at Brands Hatch, the critics began, quietly, to eat their words. Only two weeks later, at Thruxton, James became the BTCC's youngest ever race winner, coped with the sudden gush of accolades with gracious maturity - and, must have seen that the critics were now wearing the pained looks of indigestion sufferers as they swallowed their sentences whole.

Even before his Thruxton victory, Thompson made the matter-of-fact observation: 'If you can do reasonably well in a Privateer machine, there's a very good chance you'll go well in a works car.'

James Kaye agrees: 'When you

remember that Privateers have very limited resources, they're doing a very good job.' To emphasise this point, Kaye recalls, only half-joking, 'My

Right: The three leading competitors in the 1995 Total Cup share the prize cheque

Typical close Total Cup Racing at Donington Park

entire 1994 budget was less than Alfa Romeo's espresso bill.'

Perhaps because of these financial limitations - which put beyond reach the latest specification engines, or most recent suspension or chassis or brake system tweaks, or test programmes, or development engineers - Privateers only twice broke into the top ten during 1994. But in 1995 they sprung surprises.

In only the third race of the season, in pouring rain on the Brands Hatch Indy circuit, Total Cup newcomer Charlie Cox (Thames Ford Racing Team Ford Mondeo) stormed through from 21st place on the grid to fifth, spun to a halt, twice stalled his engine, rejoined in 12th, and charged back to fifth. Cox had gambled on wet weather tyres, while others slithered helplessly on slicks, but even so, with the season barely started, already the other Privateers were wondering: How can I possibly follow that?

But follow it they did. Also in slippery conditions, which this time favoured those brave enough to start

on intermediate tyres or slicks, Richard Kaye (Mint Motorsport Ford Mondeo) placed fifth in round 20 at Snetterton - and Robb Gravett (Foesport Ford Mondeo) was two places ahead of him. In the history of 2-litre BTCC racing, Gravett's stands as the best ever Privateer result.

Not that the Total Cup runners always needed difficult track conditions or a race of attrition to make their mark. A couple of hours after Gravett's third place finish, Matt Neal (Team Dynamics Ford Mondeo) went out onto a dry track and, in an entirely conventional race, started fifth on the grid and placed fourth. Neal crossed the line fully 12 seconds in front of the next car - and ahead of both works Fords.

When, at season's end, Ford's Paul Radisich tested Neal's car, he was surprised to find it running to bog-standard 1994 specification. No trick suspension geometry, no plated diff, none of the works team's big brake pads and discs, nothing more potent than an ordinary customer engine. And although Team Dynamics are the most professional outfit yet seen in the Total Cup, slick in organisation and smart in appearance, they competed on a budget so tight it would have squeezed the life out of any works team. In comparison to Matt's, a front running works car will have had four to eight times as much money lavished on it.

In addition to his strong showing at Snetterton, there were three other

occasions when Neal hustled his Mondeo to a place among the top ten qualifiers - and 22 when he was fastest qualifier among the Privateers. Matt had secured the £5000 Total Cup Flyer award by round 13 of the 25-race series - but at that stage it wasn't at all certain he'd also take the £25,000 first prize in the Total Cup, as he shared the lead with Richard Kaye and was merely six points ahead of Nigel Smith.

This was because Neal was fast enough to encounter trouble: At mid-season, Neal confided, 'I've decided not to make myself such an easy target any more, and just make sure I bring home maximum Total Cup points in the next few meetings.'

This Neal did, so that in the end he amassed 14 Total Cup victories, a tally which towered above all others. Nigel Smith (Team HMSO Vauxhall Cavalier) scored four victories, equalling his score of the previous year, when he'd finished runner-up to James Kaye; James' brother Richard took three wins, one despite a broken leg, to become this year's runner-up; 1990 BTCC Champion Robb Gravett scored two wins; and Charlie Cox and Hamish Irvine (SCB Motorsport Peugeot 405) claimed one Privateer victory apiece.

Cox and Gravett could have featured strongly, but Cox missed 11 races while recuperating from head and eye injuries sustained in that infamous aerobatics display at Thruxton (six to eight barrel rolls), and Gravett missed 12 rounds, after an unsatisfactory start to the year in an elderly Cavalier, while searching for a competitive car. In the 1995 Total Cup, that meant a Mondeo.

Suitably equipped, Gravett returned to use the Total Cup as a shopfront for his abilities. Which is, of course, the point.

The Teams

The quality of the Teams in the Auto Trader BTCC improves year on year – here is our guide to the winners and losers of '95

Vauxhall Sport
4, 10, 14, 24

Vauxhall Sport

The Vauxhall Sport Cavaliers were run by Ray Mallock Ltd and they came away with the season's biggest prize, the drivers' title.

The team has been strengthened over the past two years to the point where it is the equal of any in the BTCC. Restructuring meant that Ray Mallock himself moved away from a hands-on race-engineering role to oversee the effort, acting as team manager as well as supervising design and engineering. Daryl Cozens is the operations manager.

The Graham Humphreys-designed Cavaliers' consistent speed and reliability played a crucial part in John Cleland's victory and were a credit to the team.

On the engineering side, ex-Tyrrell F1 man Phil Barker forged an excellent relationship with Cleland, to ensure that the number 4 Cavalier was, if not the fastest car everywhere at least the car that was closest to the pace most often.

Keith Knott, formerly a long-term Indycar engineer and designer with Lola joined up to engineer the second car driven initially by James Thompson

and then by Jeff Allam and South African champion Mike Briggs.

Rob Gustavsson, another with massive single-seater experience headed the sub-assembly division and along with his team of technicians deserves real credit for the Cavaliers' reliability - Cleland suffered no retirements due to mechanical failures.

If you then note that RML produced a total of 10 1995-spec Cavaliers/Opel Vectras, built the prototype 1996 Vectra and moved from it's long-time workshops in a farmyard near Milton Keynes to a new 20,000 square foot facility 14 miles away in Wellingborough, the feat is even more remarkable. It was a superb achievement.

Williams Renault Dealer Racing

An impressive first year for the new Williams touring car arm, which netted the manufacturers' title. An entirely new enterprise, separate from the Grand Prix operation, under team director Ian Harrison, the squad soon settled into its stride.

While Harrison ran the business, the

technical side was in the hands of ex-Williams F1 engineer John Russell, who reported to team technical director Patrick Head.

The start-up to first race schedule was tight and ultimately the team's 1995 cars were not finished until just before the season opened. There were perhaps a few more early-season reliability problems than the team would have wanted, but a superb late season run in which the blue Lagunas won seven of the last nine races to haul up to first in the manufacturers' championship gave us a taste of what they'll be aiming for in 1996.

The team mix included ex-Williams F1 men like Harrison and Russell and stacks of experienced touring car men. Harrison himself was having a second bite at the BTCC, having managed the Prodrive-run works BMW team back in 1992 and members of that team to join him at Williams included team manager Dick Goodman and Alain Menu's race engineer Mark Ellis. Will Hoy was initially engineered by ex-F3 man Chris Gorne, but he left after the third meeting of the year at Thruxton. Russell filled the breach until Greg Wheeler arrived from Mitsubishi Ralliart to take

charge of Will's car from the Silverstone Grand Prix meeting.

Volvo 850 Racing

From the way the TWR-run Volvo squad started the season, you would be hard pressed to spot that it had only one year of Super Touring experience behind it. Under race director Roger Sillman the team put in more pre-season testing than anyone else and really hit the ground running at the opening races.

It was the only works team using Dunlop tyres and it's hard to tell how much this affected performances for better or worse, although Rickard Rydell's 13 poles made it clear that over a single lap they certainly weren't lacking anything.

The engineering side of the team was run by John Gentry, who also acted as race engineer on Rydell's car. Gentry has an unusually varied background having worked on everything from Formula 1 to 500cc Grand Prix motorbikes. Dave Kelly, another ex-F1 man was Tim Harvey's race engineer, interestingly Kelly also knows a bit about the Vauxhall Cavalier, having

worked on the 1994 incarnation of the BTCC's old soldier at Ray Mallock Ltd.

Team management was handled, as in 1994, by Ken Page and Charlie Bamber took over responsibility for engine development from Kiwi Allan Scott, who's returned to NZ.

The Volvo 850 Racing programme was originally scheduled to run for three years, with championship victory planned in year three. Sillman and his crew came very close to achieving the goal a year early and they'll be even more determined to take the title in 1996.

Valvoline Team Mondeo

The biggest change at Team Mondeo this year, was Andy Rouse's move from team boss/driver to team boss only, but as Andy himself says, the difference was not great. 'During the week there was really no change, while at the weekends I suppose I just had a bit more thinking time. The good thing is that I don't have to spend time in the gym any more...'

Still by and large it was a disappointing season for the Ford men,

although Rouse reckons that his team probably put in more effort over the year than any other.

The key technical staff working for Rouse - himself very much a hands-on engineer - were designer Roger King, recruited from TWR over the winter, and engineers Vic Drake and John Dorrans.

Drake is Rouse's partner in Andy Rouse Engineering and looked after Paul Radisich's car, while Dorrans ran Kelvin Burt's.

Team Toyota GB

The Toyota squad was another which made great strides towards the end of the season. Toyota GB competitions manager Paul Risbridger also acts as team manager, but the cars were run by TOM'S GB.

Indeed the whole programme's structure was altered for 1995, with World Rally Championship outfit Toyota Team Europe being recruited in a research and development role. TTE received a substantial budget straight from Japan and designed and built the Carinas used for most of the season.

However the car which showed most

Volvo 850 Racing
9, 15

Valvoline
Team Mondeo
3, 33

promise was the TOM'S-developed right-hand drive Carina which appeared for the last three meetings. Alastair McQueen was the project manager for the compact TOM'S effort and also engineered Tim Sugden's car. Stuart Ayling was the engineer for Julian Bailey, while Ewan Cameron was the TOM'S engine man and responsible for an improved power unit which also appeared at the end of the year. With just 17 personnel, including motor-home staff it was again one of the smaller operations, but full of potential.

BMW Team Motorsport

It was all-change at BMW for 1995, with the efficient and successful Team Schnitzer being re-deployed to the German Super Touring Cup, which it won with '93 BTCC king Jo Winkelhock, and replaced by BMW M Gmbh's own Nurburgring-based motorsport team, which had taken the '94 German crown with Johnny Cecotto.

Schnitzer was a tough act to follow and the 1995 318i was probably the least competitive works BMW fielded

in the BTCC in a decade, so team director Gunter Warthofer and his crew had a character-building season.

Like Schnitzer in 1994, Warthofer's squad worked from its German HQ, and this probably led to them testing a little less often than was ideal early in the season. Later in the year a separate test team, run by Ralph Bellamy and Marc Surer was set up at Silverstone. The car was certainly improved by the end of the season, but the pay-off in results terms was not significant.

Martin Moosleitner was in charge of engineering and was also the race engineer on Johnny Cecotto's car, while Jurgen `JJ' Jungklaus looked after David Brabham.

Further re-structuring of BMW's Super Touring efforts is due for 1996 and how this effects the BTCC programme is so far unclear.

Honda Team MSD

This year's only new factory team was highly impressive. Motor Sport Developments have a long and successful history in rallying and had already produced a Super Touring Opel Astra that was capable of

winning outside the BTCC, but this year David Whitehead and his crew took on a huge task.

As well as running Honda UK's two-car BTCC team MSD designed and built the new Accord Super Touring car and supplied vehicles for the German and Belgian programmes.

There are 30 people employed full-time at MSD and only six were brought in for the new Honda project so it was not, as many imagined, a question of building a whole new team, more a well-established company building on an existing infrastructure.

Whitehead, who comes from an engineering background, is MSD's managing director, but the cars are designed by former F1 BRM man and hillclimb chassis expert Mike Pilbeam, who has worked on a sub-contract basis for MSD for nearly 10 years.

The incoming six are four experienced touring car technicians plus engineer Eddie Hinckley and team manager Rod Benoist. Hinckley and Benoist followed the same route to MSD - working for TWR (Hinckley was one of Tom Walkinshaw's very first employees) before moving to

Williams Renault Dealer Racing **2, 22**

Honda
Team MSD
20, 21

Total Team
Peugeot
8, 18

Team Toyota **11, 12**

BMW Team
Motorsport
16, 17

Alfa Romeo
Old Spice Racing
1, 5, 55

Team HMSO **25**

Mint Motorsport **23**

Team Dynamics **77**

SCB Motorsport **26**

Thames Ford Dealer Team **19**

Foesport **27**

Roy Kennedy Racing **30**

Irvine aims to be back again in 1996, hoping to acquire a new Peugeot 406 in which to run his current engine and gearbox.

Robb Gravett returned to the BTCC as a privateer, aiming to regain works driver status and despite a fragmented year became the first privateer to secure a podium finish, with a superb performance at Snetterton. Robb's season got off to a false start with a short liaison with Roy Kennedy Racing and a Vauxhall Cavalier. That lasted just one meeting and Gravett did not reappear until the British Grand Prix support race.

In the meantime a new team - Foesport - had been set up and a Ford Mondeo found and rebuilt by Andy Rouse. The team's employees were Kevin Maxted, who with his own company Maxted Motorsport had run '94 Total Cup Champion James Kaye, and two mechanics, while former BTCC racer Jerry Mahony took a marketing role.

Team Magic **32**

Gravett probably spoke for almost all the privateers when he explained some of the problems of running as an independent: 'You wouldn't believe how difficult it is. We had a shoestring budget, virtually no spares and we couldn't afford new tyres for testing, which makes it virtually impossible to make the best of them in qualifying.'

Setting up a new outfit mid-season added to the difficulties: 'We had to find a car, then the people to run it, a trailer and so on. The mechanics worked incredibly hard, but they were also having to learn the car. In the end I'm pleased I did it. It was the right thing to do, but once you go fast you want to do it all the time.'

Robb certainly went fast at Snetterton, but persistent handling problems stemming from a big startline shunt in the second Snetterton race proved frustrating thereafter.

Charlie Cox was another who had a fragmented season. 'It was both the

best and the worst season of my career,' says Charlie. A sparkling start to the year, including a superb fifth place overall in the wet at Brands Hatch paled into insignificance when an horrific roll at Thruxton destroyed the car and rendered Charlie unfit to race for the next six meetings.

Charlie's Thames Ford Dealers/Evening Standard/Carphone Warehouse team had been formed in 1994 to run a Group N Escort Cosworth, with a view to BTCC graduation. Cox and Ian Cross are the team principles, with Bradley Joyce as chief mechanic and Charlie's wife Jacqui handling admin. And its effectiveness was proved by the competitiveness of the, unique in Britain, hatchback Mondeo it built up to replace the crashed ex-Radisich saloon. That was competitive almost immediately and Charlie led the privateers for quite a while in both the season's final two races at Silverstone. Charlie aims to be back for another crack in 1996.

Finally, Slim Borgudd was entered for the first few meetings in a Roger Dowson run Mazda 323, but the car failed to arrive for official qualifying,

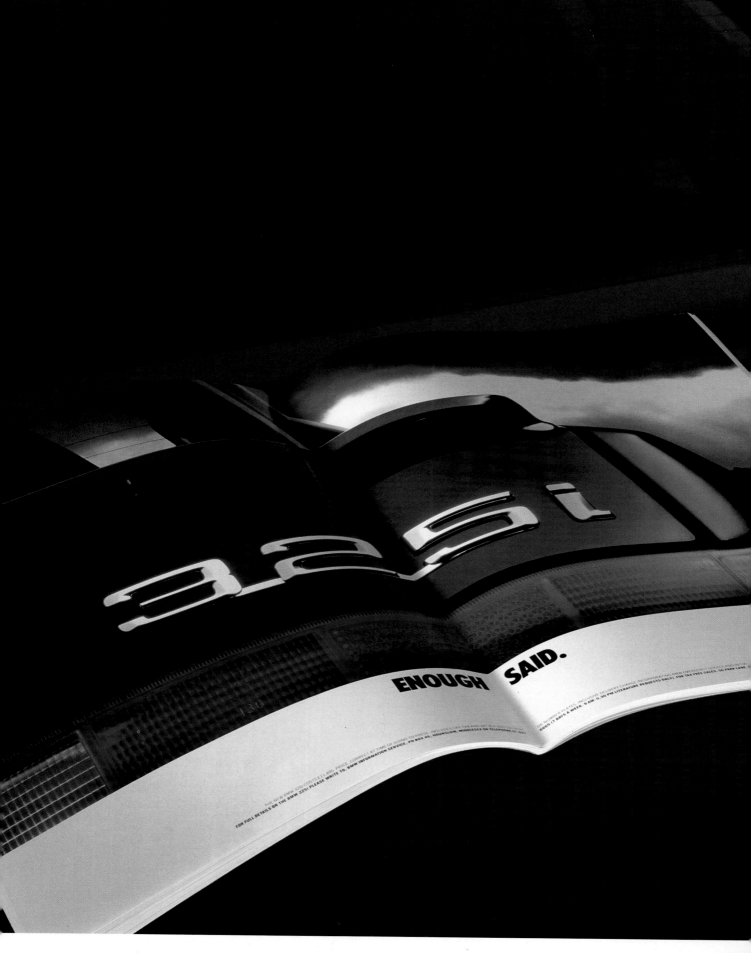

ENOUGH SAID.

THE NEW BMW 325i COSTS £19,490. PRICE, CORRECT AT TIME OF GOING TO PRESS, INCLUDES VAT AND MAY VARY AT DEALERS.
FOR FULL DETAILS ON THE BMW 325i PLEASE WRITE TO: BMW INFORMATION SERVICE, PO BOX 46, HOUNSLOW, MIDDLESEX OR TELEPHONE 01-897

UNTIL NOW

Ten years ago BMW launched the 325i and everyone was lost for words.

The badge said it all. A 2.5 litre fuel-injected straight six in a 3 Series BMW.

An engine destined to make this BMW one of the most coveted cars ever.

But time, as they say, stands still for no one. Even for the driver of a BMW 325i.

Sooner or later something even better

THAT IS.

comes along. Something with an increased capacity to please.

Something that's lighter and therefore more responsive. Something that's not just easy to drive but easier on the environment as well. Something that is, in anyone's book, the epitome of refined engineering. Enough said?

THE ULTIMATE DRIVING MACHINE

Victory for the Vs

Vauxhall's John Cleland and Volvo's Rickard Rydell flicked a V-sign to the rest. But the new wing regulations proved a contentious issue, as pundits blamed dull racing on the new spoilers

Donington Park
Rounds 1 & 2

Clockwise from left:
Rickard Rydell took two poles and one win for Volvo, here he leads Paul Radisich (3), Alain Menu (2) and the gang. Cleland took one win and the championship lead. Derek Warwick had a frustrating time on his BTCC debut. David Brabham contemplates life with BMW. Bailey kerb-hopping in the Carina.

Donington Park
Rounds 1&2

Clockwise from left:
Ladbrokes and betting mania came to the BTCC and with them a visit from Channel 4's racing expert John McCririck, here talking to commentator Brian Jones (right). Revelation James Thompson chases Hoy and Harvey. TWR celebrates Rydell's win. Cecotto's BMW dices with Leslie's promising new Honda

Honda scores points in its BTCC debut, thanks to James Kaye's 10th place in race two. Fourth in the morning warm-up for David Leslie gives the new team cause for further optimism.

After a winter of hype and build-up, it was time to raise the curtain on the brave new world of wings and splitters for all. And as far as first nights go, it wasn't a success. `Where's the overtaking?' cried the critics. `Wait and see,' demurred the drivers themselves. `let's get used to it first.'

But the fact was, the first time out anyway, that shorter braking distances and higher speeds through the faster corners had removed many of the more opportunistic - read reckless? - trademark moves of the BTCC.

In race one, John Cleland's Vauxhall made the better start from pole-sitter Rickard Rydell's Volvo and led into Redgate, followed by Alain Menu's Renault and Paul Radisich's Ford. Yep, Rydell's start had been that bad...

`I was on the limiter as the lights turned green,' said the embarrassed Swede, `and just bogged down.'

Into the Esses for the first couple of laps, Menu took a look at Cleland. But soon the Cavalier was beginning to eke out a gap to the chasing pack. At the chequered flag, Cleland came in nearly six seconds to the good over the Swiss.

`I had a good start,' recounted Cleland, `but my mirrors were full of Menu for the opening three or four laps. I tried hard for the first eight, then eased off as he began to fade a little.'

With Menu, Radisich and Rydell

bunched, but static, in the second to fourth spots, Johnny Cecotto's BMW supplied some mild excitement with a charge to fifth.

Aside from that, there were precious few overtaking manoeuvres, bar Will Hoy's ill-fated attempt to take Cecotto at the Melbourne hairpin which resulted in Julian Bailey's Toyota playing the part of involuntary backstop.

Rydell managed to match revs, clutch and lights for the start of race two and took a lead he would keep until the end. By the end of lap two, the Swede had already broken the tow to Menu, Radisich and Cleland behind, and after that, it was merely a case of nurturing the gap.

`I pushed hard for the first two laps,' said a relieved Rydell afterwards, first race faux pas annulled, `but after that, I knocked a second off my pace.' That's dominant.

Behind, Cleland had managed to take third from Radisich, with Harvey quickly following him through and Hoy taking his turn to demote the Kiwi's ill-handling Ford to sixth soon after.

Nearer the front again, Cleland and Harvey were able to move up one further place each when Menu was unable to fight growing understeer and hold the Vauxhall/Volvo coupling back at the same time.

Cleland's win and a second put him into an early lead in the points table, with Rydell second. But without that poor first start for the Swede, the impression was that things could have been significantly different.

Rickard Rydell takes a pair of poles on the debut of the Volvo 850 saloon, then gives Volvo its first ever BTCC race win.

James Thompson qualifies his Vauxhall third for race two - his second ever as a works driver - and finishes seventh in both races.

Derek Warwick's BTCC debut with Alfa Romeo ends in frustration with a trip into the McLeans barriers.

Matt Neal makes a clean sweep in the Total Cup for privateers, taking two poles and two victories.

Donington Park
Round 1 - 18 Laps

1	J Cleland	Vauxhall
2	A Menu	Renault
3	P Radisich	Ford
4	R Rydell	Volvo
5	J Cecotto	BMW
6	W Hoy	Renault
7	J Thompson	Vauxhall
8	T Harvey	Volvo
9	T Sugden	Toyota
10	G Simoni	Alfa Romeo

Fastest Lap: J Cleland
Total Cup: M Neal

Round 2 - 18 Laps

1	R Rydell	Volvo
2	J Cleland	Vauxhall
3	T Harvey	Volvo
4	A Menu	Renault
5	W Hoy	Renault
6	P Radisich	Ford
7	J Thompson	Vauxhall
8	J Cecotto	BMW
9	G Simoni	Alfa Romeo
10	J Kaye	Honda

Fastest Lap: R Rydell
Total Cup: M Neal

PHOTOGRAPHY: AUTOSPORT, BOTHWELL

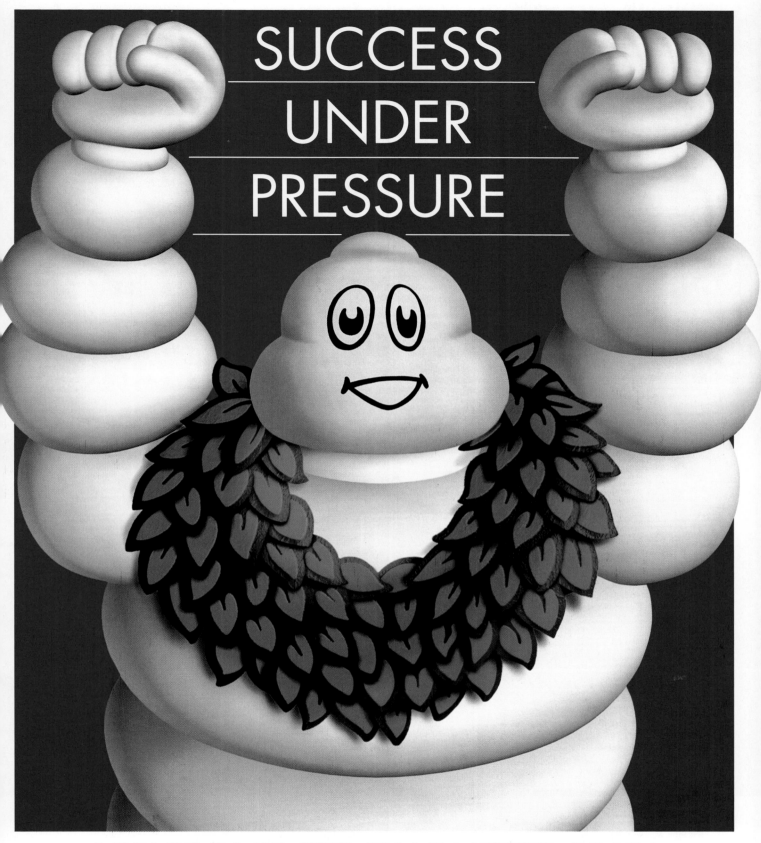

SUCCESS UNDER PRESSURE

MICHELIN PILOTS FLY IN FIRST AGAIN.

For the second year running, Michelin Pilot tyres have taken top honours in the British Touring Car Championship. John Cleland in the Vauxhall Cavalier won the drivers' championship and Alain Menu and Will Hoy in the Renault Lagunas won the constructors' title on Pilots. Fit Pilots to your car and you'll benefit from the same investment in technology that led to this sporting achievement. For more information about Pilot tyres, contact your local dealer.

MICHELIN
Pilot

PHOTOGRAPHY: AUTOSPORT, ACTION IMAGES, SIMON HILDREW

Harvey's rainstorm

Tim Harvey got on with the job of winning both races as those around him took the chance to go crazy in the rain

Clockwise from left:
The stranded wrecks of Paul Radisich (3)
and Patrick Watts prompted red flag
number two. Cleland led then crashed out
in both races. Derek Warwick's Alfa 155
was in the wars again. Hamish Irvine
ditches his privateer Peugeot 405

Clockwise from bottom left:
Menu passes a spinning Charlie Cox - the Aussie privateer was a stunning fifth in race one. Cleland slams into the Paddock barrier in race two. Tim Harvey celebrates his double win - it would be the highlight of his season

PHOTOGRAPHY: AUTOSPORT, BOTHWELL, SUTTON, ALLSPORT

Clockwise from bottom left:
A misted screen wrecked Rydell's first race. The Fords made the right tyre choice in race one and zapped up into the top three. Second and a crash for Radisich. The Williams Renault house of horrors. Two more poles for Rydell, but no more race wins

Rickard Rydell takes two more pole positions for Volvo, making it three out of four.

PHOTOGRAPHY: AUTOSPORT, JED LEICESTER, ZOOOM

After the damp squib of Donington's season-opener, Brands Hatch saw a return to form for the BTCC. The brewing controversy over wings and overtaking was forgotten as rain and some inspired tyre choices, plus some fairly crazy driving from the points leaders, gave the sodden crowd the most unpredictable pair of races seen in years.

At the end of it all, Volvo's Tim Harvey had further cemented his *rainmeister* status with a pair of excellent victories, and leapt to the top of the points standings.

Meanwhile, the pace-setters from Donington, John Cleland and Rickard Rydell, suffered mixed fortunes. Cleland left the Kent track without adding to his points after falling off at every available opportunity, while the Swede could only manage a third in race two after screen misting problems in race one.

Race one saw the first drops of rain in the London region for 20 days begin to fall just minutes before the start. It wasn't enough to declare the race wet. But it did add a confusing dimension that was quickly resolved when privateer Nigel Smith found himself stranded on the Druids kerb, bringing out the red flags.

With the rain now faster, the race was declared wet for the restart. Most chose intermediates, but Volvo, Ford, BMW's David Brabham and privateer Charlie Cox all chose full wets.

At the restart, Cleland led again, as he had in the first start. But again, just like the first start, he ran wide, allowing the Volvos through, then compounded his error with an off at Paddock - race one over for the Scot.

A theme quickly developed, with the five wet-shod works cars - in the order Rydell, Harvey, Brabham, Kelvin Burt and Paul Radisich - leading the bewildered intermediate runners, and Cox catching fast.

Charlie Cox takes highest ever privateer finishing position in race one, with fifth overall. Matt Neal wins the Total Cup class in race two.

Cox's progress was nothing short of staggering, and on lap five, he was sixth. `The opening laps went like a dream, and I couldn't help making places,' he recalled afterwards.

Now Brabham began to fade, with both works Fords passing him. But a spin for Cox, forcing him into another astonishing recovery drive, prevented the BMW driver from losing another place.

On lap 10, Harvey was past Rydell, quickly followed by Radisich, who had already been allowed to shift up a position by his team mate Burt. Two laps later, Rydell was into the pits, the victim of a misted windscreen.

Kelvin Burt scored his first points of the season with one third and one fourth.

At the flag, Harvey was almost six seconds to the good over Radisich and keen to kill off one myth: `I think this disproves the theory that Michelin wets are better than our Dunlops,' grinned the Volvo man.

Race two saw Cleland take another early lead, but again the red flags flew when Radisich and Patrick Watts's Peugeot made heavy contact on the pit straight.

At the restart, Cleland took the lead yet again, with Rydell in pursuit. But going into Surtees for the first time, an altercation between the two leaders saw Cleland off, Rydell delayed and Harvey into the lead again.

Harvey led until the flag again, chased by James Thompson's Vauxhall. But he had the red flags to thank for his victory, since the stoppage allowed him to take up his rightful grid slot after suffering starter motor problems shortly before the first start.

There was one further moment of drama when Cleland rejoined the fray, just ahead of Harvey, but almost immediately threw his Vauxhall off at Paddock with brake failure, the legacy of his off.

`I think John had the red mist descend again,' said Harvey. `No I didn't,' responded Cleland. `I just wanted to get back on, and I didn't even know it was him.'

Brands Hatch
Round 3 - 25 Laps

1	T Harvey	Volvo
2	P Radisich	Ford
3	K Burt	Ford
4	D Brabham	BMW
5	C Cox	Ford
6	J Bailey	Toyota
7	A Menu	Renault
8	P Watts	Peugeot
9	W Hoy	Renault
10	G Simoni	Alfa Romeo

Fastest Lap: P Radisich
Total Cup: C Cox

Round 4 - 27 Laps

1	T Harvey	Volvo
2	J Thompson	Vauxhall
3	R Rydell	Volvo
4	K Burt	Ford
5	J Cecotto	BMW
6	D Brabham	BMW
7	W Hoy	Renault
8	J Bailey	Toyota
9	A Menu	Renault
10	T Sugden	Toyota

Fastest Lap: K Burt
Total Cup: M Neal

Pole-master

Rickard Rydell sat on pole position for over half 1995's BTCC rounds and his tally of 13 poles was over twice as many as anyone else managed. So what's the secret? Rickard explained.

'There's no secret. With John Gentry (chief engineer at Volvo 850 Racing and Rickard's race engineer) I've found a really good set-up for one quick lap and we've worked out how to use the softer tyres well - how to make those small adjustments to keep a good balance with two softer tyres on the front of the car.

'Sometimes qualifiers are not faster than the race tyres anyway and so it is better to choose six race tyres. We've generally made the right decision about which tyres to choose.

'I also think that the Dunlops (Volvo was the only works outfit to use Dunlop tyres in '95, where most others had Michelins) are good for those two quick laps when they're new, better than Michelins I think.

'I'm happy to have been that quick, because it's very important to qualify well in the BTCC.'

Rickard must also take some of the credit personally, because he has proved himself consistently able to turn in faster qualifying laps than his team mates - last year Jan Lammers and this year, Tim Harvey.

However he must have some regrets that those 13 poles only brought him four wins. 'In a way I have, but sometimes I had mechanical problems. OK on two or three occasions my starts weren't good and I finished second or third when perhaps I should have won, but I don't think that made a crucial difference. And after I went to the Jan Lammers school of starting I had no more problems.

'Jan's starts last year were always good and so I called him up and asked him how he did it. His way was much easier and more effective. I'd been trying to start it like a Formula 3 car and it didn't work.'

Still it's been an excellent season and Rickard has hiked his status up from that of a promising mid-fielder, to one of the very best in the series. 'I'm quite happy with third and next year I hope that with more experience both the team and I will do much better.'

VOLVO

THE PORSCHE WILL BE ALO

What you see here is a Volvo 850 T-5 Estate out-accelerating a Ferrari 512 TR. It's a simple test: 50-70mph, in top gear. (The sort of acceleration you need to overtake long vehicles.)

The Volvo performs this manoeuvre in 7.2 seconds. The Ferrari does 8.2 seconds. Okay, it's only a second slower, but at 70 mph, one secon equivalent to more than 100 feet. (Or about 3 long vehicles.)

A COUPLE OF SECONDS.

The Porsche 911 Carrera isn't even in the picture. It takes a full 9.3 seconds make the trip. Fair enough, the test is in top gear, and the sports cars would t-pace the Volvo in a lower gear.

But as a measure of engine flexibility, top-gear acceleration is the yardstick (see Autocar's performance figures). Besides, how many sofas can you fit in the back of a Ferrari? **THE VOLVO 850 T-5 ESTATE. A CAR YOU CAN BELIEVE IN.**

Wins for the new boys

James Thompson became the youngest ever BTCC winner, while
Alain Menu notched up the first tin-top victory for Williams

THRUXTON CIRCUIT

Mobil
LAPS
TO GO

Thruxton
Rounds 5 & 6

Clockwise from far left:
Privateer Matt Neal qualified a superb
eighth, but lost out in this Toyota/Renault
squeeze. Cleland chases race one winner
Menu past the flag. Williams chiefs Patrick
Head (right) and Ian Harrison. Neal pops
out of the squeeze into retirement. Menu
flat out through Goodwood on his way to
victory

PHOTOGRAPHY: SUTTON, BRUCE/GRANT/BRAHAM, A&E, MICK WALKER, BOTHWELL

Thruxton
Rounds 5 & 6

Clockwise from above:
James Thompson - the BTCC's youngest
every winner at 21. Charlie Cox wrecked
his Mondeo in this 135mph roll - his injuries
kept him out of action for three months.
Johnny Cecotto takes refreshment.
Harrison chases Warwick, Sugden and the
field away from the grid. Wings at rest in
Parc Ferme

40

This was one for the record books. Vauxhall's James Thompson, at just 21-years-old, became the youngest ever winner and pole-sitter in BTCC history, while Williams Touring Car Engineering registered its first victory, with Alain Menu's Renault taking the chequered flag just five races into WTCE's debut season.

On the negative side, privateer Charlie Cox, the hero of Brands Hatch, was lucky to escape with his life after a 135mph series of barrel rolls turned his privateer Ford Mondeo into scrap metal and left him with a fractured skull and impaired vision.

Race one saw Menu convert his pole into a lead he would nurture in the opening laps, but then see being slowly whittled away by a Vauxhall drafting duo led by John Cleland, with Thompson right behind.

By lap 14, the duo had latched onto Menu, to become a loose trio, ahead of Patrick Watts's Peugeot. But on lap 16 Thompson had the Thruxton nightmare scenario of his tyre blowing at high-speed. It wasn't an isolated incident, since both Kelvin Burt's Ford and Derek Warwick's Alfa

succumbed too. Fortunately, all escaped injury, despite Burt going on a wild ride into the `boonies'.

At the chequered flag, Cleland had cut the gap to the winning Renault to just 0.33 seconds, but Menu professed to being not unduly troubled.

`John was a bit better under the brakes,' he surmised, `but I always had the inside covered. I'm just glad it wasn't another couple of laps.'

`I enjoyed it,' said Cleland. `I just hope I can turn the tables on Alain in the next race.'

Come the next race, Cleland couldn't turn the tables, but Vauxhall could, courtesy of Thompson.

Thompson took an early lead at the lights, followed by Menu, Rickard Rydell - in a strangely quiet weekend for the early-season pace-setters - and Burt's repaired Mondeo.

Going into the Club chicane, Charlie Cox's privateer Mondeo locked a brake, got on the dirt, dug in, flipped, then rolled a massive 11 times. Not surprisingly, the race was stopped while the extremely fortunate Aussie was extricated.

At the restart, Thompson did it again, taking a lead ahead of Menu and Burt. Over the course of the next dozen laps, the Swiss didn't once lay off the pressure on the unfazed Vauxhall youngster, but still the pair maintained enough pace to pull clear of Burt and Rydell.

In the final stages, Thompson at last

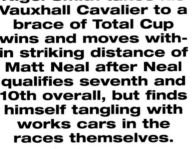

Nigel Smith takes his Vauxhall Cavalier to a brace of Total Cup wins and moves within striking distance of Matt Neal after Neal qualifies seventh and 10th overall, but finds himself tangling with works cars in the races themselves.

Tim Sugden takes Toyota's best finish of the season so far with fourth in race one.

began to put air between himself and the Renault and took the chequered by 2.85s. `I edged away,' said Thompson, `and then just concentrated on looking after my tyres.'

`I saved my tyres too,' said Menu, `and thought about the championship.' Which was no bad thing, since the first and the second had made him the latest driver to take the points lead.

Burt came in third, ahead of Rydell and a delayed Cleland, who had banged wheels with Patrick Watts through Segrave and emerged much the better of the two.

Will Hoy takes a front row slot for Renault in race two, but fails to start after steering rack problems.

Touring car year 95-96

Thruxton
Round 5 - 20 Laps

1	A Menu	Renault
2	J Cleland	Vauxhall
3	P Watts	Peugeot
4	T Sugden	Toyota
5	D Brabham	BMW
6	G Simoni	Alfa Romeo
7	J Bailey	Toyota
8	D Leslie	Honda
9	R Rydell	Volvo
10	S Harrison	Peugeot

Fastest Lap: A Menu
Total Cup: N Smith

Round 6 - 17 Laps

1	J Thompson	Vauxhall
2	A Menu	Renault
3	K Burt	Ford
4	R Rydell	Volvo
5	J Cleland	Vauxhall
6	P Radisich	Ford
7	T Harvey	Volvo
8	J Bailey	Toyota
9	S Harrison	Peugeot
10	G Simoni	Alfa Romeo

Fastest Lap: J Thompson
Total Cup: N Smith

PARTNERS IN PERFORMANCE

FINA PLC, FINA HOUSE, ASHLEY AVENUE, EPSOM, SURREY KT18 5AD.
TELEPHONE: (01372) 726226. FAX: (01372) 744520.

PHOTOGRAPHY: AUTOSPORT, BOTHWELL, SHUTTERSPEED

Return of the Fords

After a difficult start Ford found a circuit that suited the Mondeo and Paul Radisich took his first win of the year. Volvo and Rickard Rydell also returned to winning ways

"Team Schemes"

HMSO Books

Clockwise from left:
Will Hoy takes his scootering seriously. The
Mondeo shone and Radisich won round
eight. Patrick Watts spits flame on his way
to sixth and 10th places. Richard Kaye eats
gravel. John Cleland and Vauxhall boss
Mike Nicholson celebrate the Scot's 100th
BTCC start. Total Cup man Nigel Smith
looks mean

With its long straights and selection of slow and medium speed corners, the Silverstone National circuit was ideal for the Ford's V6 power - and would also help to conceal the Mondeo's penchant for eating its tyres.

Two poles for Rydell was pretty much business as usual, but a Ford two-three in the first qualifying session - with Kelvin Burt getting the better of Radisich - and second on the grid for Radisich in the second session pointed to a day of possibilities for the Blue Oval.

At the start of race one, Rydell belied his reputation as a slow starter and led Radisich into Copse - but not out of it as the Swede corrected for oversteer and Radisich dived through into the lead.

For the next 21 and three-quarters laps out of the total of 25, Radisich held off the Volvo's attack, thanks to superior grunt on the straight heading off the Volvo's better brakes and cornering abilities.

`But I guess I overworked my tyres,' rued Radisich. And finally, exiting Becketts for the 22nd time, Rydell got his chance.

`I could see his tyres going off,' explained Rydell, `I was better out of the corner, went side-by-side down the straight and got him on the inside into Brooklands.'

With a clear track ahead of him, Rydell pulled out 1.5s by the flag, with Radisich a further 6.16s ahead of John Cleland's Vauxhall, which had never quite got to grips with the National circuit. Cleland's team mate James Thompson was in similar trouble, but nevertheless fought his Cavalier to fourth place.

Burt's hopes were soon dashed - he'd been forced out of the proceedings at an early stage after taking a

hit from Tim Sugden's Toyota. `I got a run on him,' said Sugden, `but I just hit him.'

In race two, Radisich made good use of his front row slot to outdrag Rydell at the lights. Burt nipped into second, but found the Ford supremacy short-lived as the red flags flew after a first corner clash between Patrick Watts' Peugeot, David Brabham's BMW and Julian Bailey's Toyota at Copse.

At the restart, Radisich again led into Copse, but this time chased by Rydell, ahead of Burt.

For four laps, Radisich worked hard to put a 1.6s gap between himself and Rydell. Then slowly, but surely, the Volvo began to fight back. This time, however, as the pair coupled together in the closing laps, Radisich managed to find

enough in reserve to hold the menacing Volvo at bay.

`I knew he'd catch me,' said Radisich, `but I'd rested my tyres in the middle of the race and he'd worked his hard, so I had enough left to hold him off at the end.'

Burt had held on to third in the

opening laps, but his tyre-led decline was swift when it finally happened. At the chequered flag, Tim Harvey's Volvo, Alain Menu's Renault, Cleland and Sugden had all got the better of the ailing Ford. `The car got worse and worse,' grimaced Burt, `and I just became a sitting duck.'

Rydell retakes the points lead with his first and second. Cleland's third and fifth puts him second in the points after Menu can only salvage one fourth from the weekend.

David Leslie takes third on the grid for race two - Honda's best qualifying performance of the year and backs that up with points for ninth and then eighth places.

PHOTOGRAPHY: AUTOSPORT, SUTTON, BRYN WILLIAMS

Touring car year 95-96

Silverstone
Round 7 - 25 Laps

1	R Rydell	Volvo
2	P Radisich	Ford
3	J Cleland	Vauxhall
4	J Thompson	Vauxhall
5	W Hoy	Renault
6	P Watts	Peugeot
7	T Harvey	Volvo
8	D Brabham	BMW
9	D Leslie	Honda
10	J Kaye	Honda

Fastest Lap: P Radisich
Total Cup: M Neal

Round 8 - 22 Laps

1	P Radisich	Ford
2	R Rydell	Volvo
3	T Harvey	Volvo
4	A Menu	Renault
5	J Cleland	Vauxhall
6	T Sugden	Toyota
7	K Burt	Ford
8	D Leslie	Honda
9	G Simoni	Alfa Romeo
10	P Watts	Peugeot

Fastest Lap: P Radisich
Total Cup: M Neal

Matt Neal puts Thruxton behind him and takes a pair of victories in the Total Cup as Nigel Smith's challenge falters with a pair of mechanical retirements.

SUNDAY SPORT HAS NEVER BEEN FILTHIER.

For further information on the Peugeot 106 Rallye, contact your local dealer or call 0500 500 106.

106
PEUGEOT

THE PEUGEOT 106 RALLYE.

No passing zone?

It was close, but where was the passing? Rickard Rydell and Alain Menu led the high-speed processions at Oulton Park

PHOTOGRAPHY: AUTOSPORT, SUTTON, BOTHWELL, BRYN WILLIAMS, SHUTTERSPEED

Oulton Park
Rounds 9 & 10

Clockwise from left:
James Thompson was tipped into a spin at the start of race one. Regular Oulton star Alain Menu won race two. Derek Warwick was briefly knocked out in this race-stopping shunt. Reigning champion Gabriele Tarquini returned to join Warwick and Giampiero Simoni in a three-car Alfa attack

Oulton Park
Rounds 9 & 10

Clockwise from right:
Julian Bailey on his way to fourth place in round nine for Toyota. Radisich snatches a brief lead before round nine was red-flagged. The crowds flocked to Oulton as usual. Nigel Smith took maximum Total Cup points in the first race. James Kaye kicks up the dirt as he tries to keep the Toyotas behind his Honda.

David Leslie and Derek Warwick were involved in the race stopping accident at Island Bend in the first race.

Rickard Rydell had pointed out - had kept pointing out - that the Vauxhall Cavalier, and not his Volvo 850, was the fastest car at Oulton Park. One pole, one second on the grid, one win and one second place later, you began to doubt him.

Rydell's points haul helped him to consolidate his championship lead. But a win and a third for Alain Menu's Renault, against a second and a third for John Cleland's Vauxhall swapped the order in the battle for second in the points, with the Swiss leaping ahead of the Scot.

At the start of race one, Rydell and pole-sitter James Thompson found themselves joined by Kelvin Burt's Ford going three-abreast into Old Hall, the first corner. Thompson's Cavalier was slewed round in front of the pack, but thankfully avoided, while Burt limped little further with a broken strut.

Rydell led the pack round the lap, but behind, the Honda of David

Leslie and Derek Warwick's Alfa had tangled big time at the 100mph Island Bend. Both cars were extensively damaged and, with Warwick momentarily unconscious, the red flags flew to stop the race.

It was good news for Rydell, since Paul Radisich had just managed to monster his Ford into the lead. But at the restart, the Swede made sure he was away ahead of Cleland, Radisich and Menu. Menu was through into third

James Thompson comes back from an enormous testing shunt the day before to take his second pole position of the year, but is taken out of contention by a clash with Kelvin Burt's Ford.

Reigning BTCC champ Gabriele Tarquini returns for a one-off appearance, but twice qualifies a disappointing 19th and is taken off at the second corner in race two.

after two laps and that's how the order stayed until the end, with the top three holding close formation, but unable to make any decisive moves.

`The Vauxhall *was* the quicker car,' insisted Rydell, `but I just made my tyres last a little bit better.'

Further back, Radisich was soon out with a broken wheel, leaving Julian Bailey to take a heartening result for Toyota, ahead of Giampiero Simoni's Alfa Romeo - its best result of the season - and Thompson's smoking, limping Vauxhall.

Race two was pretty much more of the same, only with Menu taking the initiative at the start this time. Rydell followed, ahead of a repaired Burt Mondeo and Cleland and Thompson. But with Burt suffering a broken exhaust, he would soon drop back behind both Vauxhalls and team mate Radisich.

Again the race descended into a

One win apiece for runaway leader Matt Neal and Nigel Smith in the Total Cup for privateers, but consistent finishes for Richard Kaye's Mondeo bring him level on points with Smith in second overall.

static convoy at the front, with Menu taking his second win of the season with little real trouble.

`Unless you're at the front nowadays,' commented Cleland afterwards, `you don't win races nowadays.' Those wings again...

Oulton Park
Round 9 - 13 Laps

1	R Rydell	Volvo
2	J Cleland	Vauxhall
3	A Menu	Renault
4	J Bailey	Toyota
5	G Simoni	Alfa Romeo
6	J Thompson	Vauxhall
7	S Harrison	Peugeot
8	T Harvey	Volvo
9	J Cecotto	BMW
10	D Brabham	BMW

Fastest Lap: A Menu
Total Cup: N Smith

Round 10 - 16 Laps

1	A Menu	Renault
2	R Rydell	Volvo
3	J Cleland	Vauxhall
4	J Thompson	Vauxhall
5	P Radisich	Ford
6	K Burt	Ford
7	T Harvey	Volvo
8	G Simoni	Alfa Romeo
9	D Brabham	BMW
10	J Bailey	Toyota

Fastest Lap: A Menu
Total Cup: M Neal

Hopes Un-fulfilled

Derek Warwick came into the BTCC, with reigning champions Alfa Romeo at the beginning of this year, full of enthusiasm and optimism. The season turned into a nightmare, but the former F1 star hasn't been put off. He wants to come back for more in 1996.

Derek is 100% sure that he can win in the right car, he's also 1000% sure he wants to have another go at the series and believes that Prodrive would want him back 1,000,000%. He may not get far in maths evening classes, but the enthusiasm is barely dented.

So after a season which brought him more non-finishes than all but one of his rivals and fewer points than any other regular works driver, how will he remember the season? 'The overall memory,' he says, 'is going to be of frustration with the racing; fun with the racing and the fact that I enjoyed front-wheel drive much more than I expected. I really enjoyed the whole scene, getting close to the spectators and marshals and so on. There is some sadness, in that in my own mind I did as good a job with that car as was possible, but that I won't get the credit. If I'd been two 10ths off Tarquini and he'd been on pole and me third, everyone would have said I was doing a brilliant job, but down where we were two 10ths could mean 10 places.'

He does acknowledge that the bad times did eventually get to him: 'I have to say I lost heart in the last few races, because I was so frustrated, but I really want to be in the series again next year, because I want to show a few sceptics that I am good enough to win in the right material. The series is great. There are still big steps forward we can make on safety and I don't like the double races - the twin format is the way to go - but I was more than impressed with what I found. It would be a tragedy for me personally if I'm not out in a competitive car next year, because I'd love to show you all what I can do.'

Clockwise from above:
John Cleland celebrates his excellent win in
the round 11 downpour. 'Pay attention
class!' - clerk of the course Pierre
Aumonier (right) lectures the drivers on the
grid. Tim Sugden slammed into the
Clearways barrier after his screen misted
over. James Kaye crashed the Honda
heavily in qualifying.

Red rain falling down

*Three red flags, a public lambasting for the drivers and a win
apiece for Alain Menu and John Cleland in dreadful conditions
saw the BTCC balance of power shift again*

PHOTOGRAPHY: AUTOSPORT, BOTHWELL, SIMON HILDREW, DEAN POWELL

Brands Hatch
Rounds 11 & 12

Clockwise from left:

The sun shone during qualifying - Warwick chases the pack. Alain Menu took an excellent round 11 win. Cleland's pixie impression fooled no one but he went on to win round 12. Rickard Rydell abandons his heavily shunted 850 at Westfield. Radisich shows off the Mondeo's fluorescent logo

Poor old Brands Hatch. The annual blast around one of the best circuits in the world - the full Brands Grand Prix loop - and just like at the BTCC's first visit of the season, it absolutely throws it down.

By the end of the day, John Cleland had managed to take the championship lead with a first and a second in his Vauxhall, with Alain Menu's Renault right on his tail after picking up a win and a third. But for erstwhile leader Rickard Rydell, it was disaster time, with one seventh and an accident that left him on his side pushing him down to third in the points.

At the start of race one, pole-sitter Menu led the pack for the first two corners, but was challenged by James Thompson's Vauxhall on the run down from Druids. The pair banged wheels, Thompson went off, rejoined and was hit by Paul Radisich's Ford, which itself had emerged disabled from being the filling in a Volvo sandwich. Others were involved too, but the remainder headed out onto the full Grand Prix loop.

On their return, Menu led from Cleland, with the order constantly evolving behind. Then, on lap nine, the reds flew for the first time after Tim Sugden's Toyota ended up on its roof at Clearways. `The car was misting up, I couldn't see any-

Alain Menu took both poles for Renault and Williams, with both laps coming on race tyres.

thing and I hit the tyre barrier, which put me on my roof,' said a shaken, but unhurt Sugden.

A 20 minute delay, followed by a five lap sprint - results to be declared on aggregate - saw Menu take the initiative again, ahead of Cleland, Will Hoy's Renault and Tim Harvey's Volvo. It stayed like that until the end.

`I made two good starts,' said Menu, `which allowed me to pull out gaps in the early laps. After that, I knew I could hold off whoever I needed to.'

Race two saw the reds flying almost immediately, with Nigel Smith's privateer Cavalier in the Stirlings gravel. At the restart, Menu led Cleland and Thompson into th countryside. But... red flags. Rickard Rydell's Volvo was

Hamish Irvine and Richard Kaye shake up the Total Cup form with a win apiece. The second race sees the closest Total Cup finish ever, with Kaye edging Irvine by just half a car's length - two hundredths of a second.

James Kaye suffered a major off at Dingle Dell during qualifying, but was able to start after an all-night rebuild by the MSD Honda team.

Brands Hatch
Round 11 - 13 Laps

1	A Menu	Renault
2	J Cleland	Vauxhall
3	T Harvey	Volvo
4	W Hoy	Renault
5	P Watts	Peugeot
6	J Bailey	Toyota
7	R Rydell	Volvo
8	D Warwick	Alfa Romeo
9	G Simoni	Alfa Romeo
10	J Cecotto	BMW

Fastest Lap: J Cleland
Total Cup: H Irvine

Round 12 - 10 Laps

1	J Cleland	Vauxhall
2	J Thompson	Vauxhall
3	A Menu	Renault
4	W Hoy	Renault
5	T Harvey	Volvo
6	J Bailey	Toyota
7	P Radisich	Ford
8	P Watts	Peugeot
9	J Cecotto	BMW
10	D Brabham	BMW

Fastest Lap: A Menu
Total Cup: R Kaye

on its side at Westfield. Thankfully the Swede was unhurt, but on a corner that fast, it could have been a big one.

Time for a major bollocking from the clerk of the course on the grid, then start number five, with the rain even heavier now. This time Cleland was away the quickest, with his team mate Thompson shadowing him all the way to the flag. Menu was third, ahead of his team mate Hoy. But with the rain now at its heaviest, there was little call for heroics.

`It's good to be leading the points,' said a cagey Cleland afterwards, `but there's still a long, long way to go, and you've seen every week how the balance has shifted.'

Brands marked the first points for Derek Warwick since he joined the BTCC with Alfa. The former Grand Prix driver took eighth in race one, but just missed out on the double with 11th in race two.

Subscribe to the best!

10 FREE ISSUES

AUTOSPORT is the world's best motor racing magazine. Covering every aspect of motorsport - from Formula 1 to IndyCars, Le Mans to touring cars and rallying, plus all the news from the club scene - Autosport is the "bible" of motor racing. For all the news, and all the action, Autosport is an essential weekly read for everyone close to the sport.

3 FREE ISSUES

Classic and Sportscar is the UK's leading classic magazine. From Ferrari to Mini, and from Caterham to Jaguar, Classic and Sportscar covers them all, with the finest editorial and stunning photography. It is sold in over 100 countries worldwide and with advertising and cars for sale from all around the world, no other magazine gives you more.

Clockwise from right:
John Cleland sprays the champagne after dominating the weekend. This little tangle at Melbourne ended with Simoni, Watts and Warwick all out. Calm before the storm. Kelvin Burt made the podium again with third place in round 14. Hugh McCaig of Ecurie Ecosse and RML balances the silverware

TOTAL

PEUGEOT
Finance

Cleland moves clear

John Cleland consolidated his championship lead with a brilliant double victory at Donington Park. And he took his first pole positions in the BTCC for two years. It was a dominant performance

John Cleland could remember the last time he'd taken pole position - it was May 31, 1993 at Oulton Park. But now he had two more, and that was just the start of it. A mere 24 hours later, the Vauxhall ace had bagged two more wins - making it three on the trot - and increased his championship lead to 28 points.

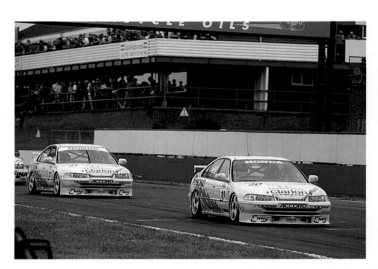

Cleland's happy weekend was compounded by some erratic form from his two closest title challengers. Second-placed Alain Menu could muster only a third and a fourth, while Rickard Rydell's second in race one was followed by a sixth in race two.

For the start of race one, Vauxhall found itself with the front row all to itself. Cleland duly leapt into the lead, but James Thompson was

unable to play the dutiful tail-gunner when he became momentarily bogged down at the lights.

Instead, it was Honda's David Leslie following Cleland around the opening lap, and actually leading momentarily on the run to the Goddard hairpin, until forced wide and down to fourth on the exit. Leslie eventually

Patrick Watts' Peugeot and the Alfas of Derek Warwick and Giampiero Simoni were all put out of race two after a tangle on the run to Goddard. Official verdict: a 50/50 ball.

Both Hondas qualified in the top 10 for both races, with Leslie's third on the grid in race one equalling his best performance of the season.

faded to seventh, but it was still another very good performance for the rookie Honda team.

Rydell and Menu loosely tailed Cleland for the rest of the race, but it was left to Thompson to supply the action at the front as he scythed his way to fourth with a series of demon outbraking moves into the Esses.

Afterwards, the buoyant Cleland was ready to do it all again. 'It took a couple of minutes to drop Rickard,'

he noted, 'but after that I kept it nice and neat and found it easy once I had the buffer.'

Sure enough at the start of race two, Cleland was away again and into a lead he would never lose. Paul Radisich kept his Ford a tight second for a while, ahead of team mate Kelvin Burt. But as Radisich pointed out: 'after a handful of laps, the Fords were struggling for traction and Cleland wasn't.'

Menu rolled in fourth, ahead of Thompson, who managed to fight off the late advances of Rydell. But there was little drama in the top group to speak about.

'I'm sorry if it wasn't exciting enough for you,' grinned Cleland unconvincingly. 'But here, my car was just perfect for the track and I couldn't really do anything but win.'

Richard Kaye won the second Total Cup race, and went into the joint lead of the points with Matt Neal, despite sporting a broken left leg - the legacy of a dog running in front of his bike. Nigel Smith won the first race, but Neal made it four non-finishes in a row.

Touring car year 95-96

Donington Park
Round 13 - 15 Laps

1	J Cleland	Vauxhall
2	R Rydell	Volvo
3	A Menu	Renault
4	J Thompson	Vauxhall
5	P Radisich	Ford
6	J Bailey	Toyota
7	D Leslie	Honda
8	T Sugden	Toyota
9	K Burt	Ford
10	T Harvey	Volvo

Fastest Lap: J Cleland
Total Cup: N Smith

Round 14 - 15 Laps

1	J Cleland	Vauxhall
2	P Radisich	Ford
3	K Burt	Ford
4	A Menu	Renault
5	J Thompson	Vauxhall
6	R Rydell	Volvo
7	J Bailey	Toyota
8	W Hoy	Renault
9	D Leslie	Honda
10	J Kaye	Honda

Fastest Lap: J Cleland
Total Cup: R Kaye

850°c
No Sweat

![Checkered flag]

THE UNIQUE RANGE
OF LIQUID COOLED BRAKE
CALIPERS FROM AP RACING

Already winning in the World Rally
Championship, DTM, BTCC and
Touring Car World Cup.

Substantial reductions in caliper
temperatures result in more consistent performance and improved life.

Simple and dependable technology.

Contact AP Racing for details.

AP Racing, Wheler Road, Seven Stars Industrial Estate, Coventry CV3 4LB. Tel: 01203 639595 International: +44 1203 639595 Fax: 01203 639559

Vauxhall's blue riband

John Cleland extended his winning streak to four on the trot with victory in the BTCC's most prestigious round, the Grand Prix support race in front of a giant crowd at Silverstone

Clockwise from left:
Cleland savours the moment. Tim Sugden battled the Carina up to eighth from 18th on the grid. Cleland and Radisich head the BTCC power-boat formation team into Copse for the first time. 'The gravel trap just jumped out,' Harvey (left) explains his retirement to Brabham (centre) and Bailey

Silverstone
Round 15

Clockwise from below:
James Thompson lost pole on a technicality, but took a fine third in the race. Advanced ventilation - the Cleland boot holds the Cavalier door open. Prodrive boss David Richards says *arrivederci* to the departing Giampiero Simoni. The fans were sad to see Giampiero go. Total Cup man Matt Neal relaxes

PHOTOGRAPHY: AUTOSPORT, SIMON HILDREW, BOTHWELL

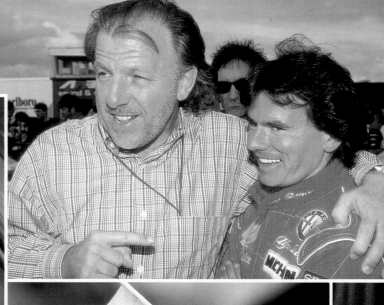

PHOTOGRAPHY: SUTTON, SIMON HILDREW, AUTOSPORT

With only one race at the end of it and a single qualifying session right at the end of each day of practice, the three-day Grand Prix meeting is a lot of `hurry up and wait' for the BTCC boys.

In the end, all that standing around was worth it for Vauxhall's John Cleland, one of the self-proclaimed GP weekend haters, when he made it four wins and three poles on the trot. In yet another wet race for the BTCC, both Alain Menu and Rickard Rydell suffered problems that left the nearest

chasers to runaway championship leader Cleland well out of the points, and suddenly it looked like a second BTCC was well within the Scot's reach.

Surprisingly enough, despite the rain coming down by the bucket only minutes before the tintops were due out, the start was free of the first corner chaos we had come to expect on the first lap of the BTCC's big day out.

Cleland led into the first corner, followed by Paul Radisich's Ford, Menu's Renault, Rydell's Volvo and Will Hoy's Renault. Radisich was soon looking at a way past the Cavalier and took the lead on the drag through the Vale, after chancing his arm on the inside at Stowe.

`I went in deep and John just kept on going wider, wider, wider,' smiled the Kiwi after-

wards. `That's because I didn't want to touch him,' added Cleland.

Cleland fought back and regained the place at Priory. But Radisich wasn't about to admit defeat and took back the lead through the Becketts complex.

Great stuff, but looking even better now that Hoy had scythed his way past Rydell and Menu, who were both suffering misting problems.

Ending lap four, Cleland dived down the inside of the Ford at Luffield and was followed through in perfect opportunist style by Hoy. Soon these two began to pull away from the rest, despite Hoy having lost his wiper blade. `With a wiper, I think I could have had John,' said Hoy, who was still glad to have turned round a hitherto dreadful first season with Renault.

With the rain now easing off, Radisich was finding it difficult to keep the rest behind him now. Tim Harvey's Volvo was quickly through, as were James Thompson's Vauxhall, Kelvin Burt's flying Ford and Julian Bailey's

Giampiero Simoni makes his last BTCC appearance for Alfa. He is to be replaced full-time by reigning champion Gabriele Tarquini from Knockhill onwards.

With 24 points on offer for a win, Cleland's championship lead of 52 points over Alain Menu means he cannot be overhauled, regardless of events at Knockhill.

Robb Gravett makes a winning return to the Total Cup, having swapped the Vauxhall Cavalier he raced in the opening round for a Ford Mondeo. Matt Neal's second in class gives him a clear points lead once again.

Charlie Cox, injured at Thruxton, is back in circulation at Silverstone and hoping to introduce his new five-door Mondeo into the fray at Brands Hatch in August.

Toyota Carina.

Soon, Thompson and Bailey were both past Harvey, and Burt looked like doing the job too. But in the end, it didn't matter, with Harvey missing his braking for Club with Burt alongside and finding the gravel instead.

With more heavy rain falling in the closing laps, Cleland's position became completely safe, thanks to Hoy's near blindness. `One more lap and I'd seriously have to have given up,' said Hoy. `I was looking for the apexes through the side window.'

Any thoughts on the title from Cleland? No, not really. `We've got 10 rounds and a lot of serious racing to go,' came the Scot's reply, `so I'm not getting complacent. And I guess I have to stop winning at some point.'

Silverstone
Round 15 - 15 Laps

1	J Cleland	Vauxhall
2	W Hoy	Renault
3	J Thompson	Vauxhall
4	J Bailey	Toyota
5	K Burt	Ford
6	P Radisich	Ford
7	D Brabham	BMW
8	T Sugden	Toyota
9	D Warwick	Alfa Romeo
10	P Watts	Peugeot

Fastest Lap: J Bailey
Total Cup: R Gravett

Keeping it clean

Peter Riches has one of the BTCC's least glamorous tasks - to make sure the series' technical regulations are complied with - but even in this area progress is relentless. So much so that from next year Peter leaves the ranks of the enthusiastic volunteer part-time experts and becomes a paid full-time employee of series organiser TOCA Ltd.

'The level of professionalism in the series continues to go up,' says Riches, 'hence the need for me to go full time. The series is generally healthy. I've had no major differences of opinion with anyone this year and we've got to a stage where people generally talk to me about what they want to do, before they do it. There are more and more engineers pushing the rules though.' One of this year's major innovations in Riches' sphere has been the recruitment of computer software specialists Liverpool Data Research Associates to check that no-one has hidden electronic driver aids. LDRA have already done a similar job in Formula 1 and their activity in the BTCC (not cheap and paid for by the teams themselves) has been very useful. 'From about the fourth race of the year we've heard no more mutterings about illegal traction control,' says Riches. 'Once people know that you have the ability to check things like electronic traction control, the problem goes away.' Along with the technical ability to regulate electronics, there has come a political desire to stop this kind of technology and its application to differentials and suspension where it is now. Various teams were starting to develop highly sophisticated systems this year, but new rulings from the sport's governing body will ensure that these potentially very expensive developments will never race, something which Riches has been very keen to ensure. Maintenance of a level playing field is essential for any race series to succeed and that essentially is Riches task. Now that he can spend more time working at it, we can expect an even more successful 1996 season.

PHOTOGRAPHY: AUTOSPORT, GRAEME BROWN, MARCO PALMIERI

Rydell and Menu thrive

A win apiece for Rickard Rydell's Volvo 850 and Alain Menu's Renault Laguna, as John Cleland and the Vauxhall Cavalier floundered on home turf, closed up the title fight once again

Mobil 1

Clockwise from left:
James Thompson escaped from this horrific shunt, which started at Duffus Dip, with relatively minor injuries, however impaired vision kept him out of racing for the rest of the season. Vauxhall old boy Jeff Allam was called in as substitute and soon found himself back in the autograph writing swing. Honda's James Kaye and an off-duty catch

Clockwise from bottom left:
Alain Menu leads into Duffus - but for a gear selection problem he should have won both races. Hamish Irvine enjoyed himself on home turf. The Menu crash hat, ready for action. Gabriele Tarquini returned to the BTCC full time at the track where he had his dramatic roll in 1994 - he stayed upright this time and even scored points

Knockhill
Rounds 16 & 17

Clockwise from above:
Knockhill from the air - the Fife circuit is in
the beautiful hills north of Dunfermline. The
TWR men ready Rydell's 850 for action.
Rydell and Harvey were on the podium for
both races. Burt was third for Ford in race
one. Matt Neal tries the popular kart track.
Cecotto starred on his way to fourth in
race one.

74

W hatever happened in Scotland, John Cleland knew he'd leave with the championship lead still intact. But with the Vauxhall refusing to play ball over the kerbs of Knockhill, and fifth and sixth all he could salvage as a result, perhaps the Scot wasn't expecting his winning streak to end in such ignominy.

In the end, Alain Menu and Rickard Rydell were the major players. Rydell took a pair of poles - his eighth and ninth of the season - and inherited victory in the first race after Menu suffered gear selection problems, while Menu could only think of what might have been as he strolled to victory in the second race.

In the first race, Rydell ended up winning almost as he pleased following Menu's demise. `I didn't get off the line very quickly, because the lights changed very quickly' recalled Rydell, whose reputation for tardy starts by now preceded him. `I was pushing hard, but Alain was very quick and only his problems made it easy for me in the end.'

Menu had dominated the early laps, getting the jump on the Volvo and never looking back until those selector problems intervened. `I was just controlling the gap,' said the disappointed Swiss, `but that's racing.'

Rydell's Volvo team mate Tim Harvey took second, some seven seconds behind, with Kelvin Burt's Ford inheriting third. But it was the guys

BTCC champion Gabriele Tarquini marks his full-time return to the championship with eighth in the second race after a potential top five is thwarted by wheel hub problems in the first.

further back supplying the real excitement, with Johnny Cecotto's BMW finishing a fighting fourth and Julian Bailey disappointed to only finish sixth for Toyota, just behind Cleland.

Menu made no mistakes in the second race and was able to pull away from Rydell and hold a near-three second lead at the chequered flag. Tim Harvey came in third, but again it was a BMW supplying the excitement, this time with David Brabham taking fourth spot for the Munich marque.

Honda backed up some strong qualifying performances with fifth for James Kaye and seventh for David Leslie in race two. `I began to struggle a bit with traction towards the end,' said Scot Leslie, `but apart from that, I think we've shown we've made serious progress.'

For his part, Cleland could only look forward to the next round and the BTCC's third and final visit to Brands

James Thompson is out for the rest of the season after a 100mph-plus testing accident at Duffus Dip leaves the youngster suffering impaired vision and heavy bruising. Former works driver Jeff Allam steps in at short notice.

Matt Neal finally returned to winning ways in the Total Cup, with both class wins going the Midlander's way. Neal shares the poles with Robb Gravett, who has to settle for a pair of seconds in the races themselves.

The rear-wheel drive BMWs are allowed to reduce their weight penalty relative to the front-wheel drive cars by 25 kilos. The reduction means a BMW now weighs in at 1000 kilos, with the rest tipping the scales at 975 kilos. In performance terms, it leads to the marque's best showing of the season.

Hatch. `I knew the streak had to end sometime,' he said, grim-faced, `but not by finishing this far back. it's been my worst meeting for a long, long time.'

Touring car year 95-96

Knockhill
Round 16 - 31 Laps

1	R Rydell	Volvo
2	T Harvey	Volvo
3	K Burt	Ford
4	J Cecotto	BMW
5	J Cleland	Vauxhall
6	J Bailey	Toyota
7	T Sugden	Toyota
8	J Allam	Vauxhall
9	M Neal	Ford
10	R Gravett	Ford

Fastest Lap: R Rydell
Total Cup: M Neal

Round 17 - 32 Laps

1	A Menu	Renault
2	R Rydell	Volvo
3	T Harvey	Volvo
4	D Brabham	BMW
5	J Kaye	Honda
6	J Cleland	Vauxhall
7	D Leslie	Honda
8	G Tarquini	Alfa Romeo
9	J Bailey	Toyota
10	T Sugden	Toyota

Fastest Lap: T Harvey
Total Cup: M Neal

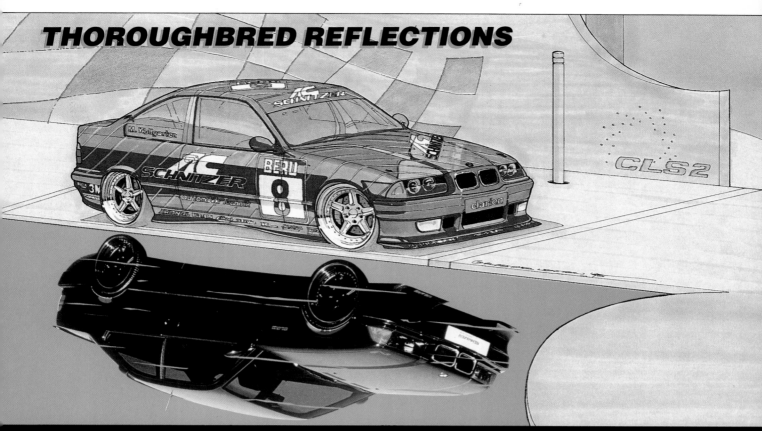

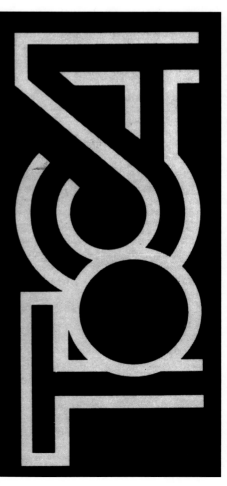

PHOTOGRAPHY: AUTOSPORT, BOTHWELL PHOTOGRAPHIC, SIMON HILDREW

The return of Hoy

It had been a tough, tough first year for Will Hoy at Renault. But finally it all came good at Brands with the '91 champ taking his first BTCC win since 1992

Brands Hatch
Rounds 18 & 19

Clockwise from above: Will Hoy heads for victory. Cecotto took a fine fifth for BMW. The privateer gang - Neal, Gravett and Smith - hard at it. Concentration from Tarquini, Russo and Richards - it brought a fourth place in race two. Radisich fends off the fans with pen and programme. Hip hip Hoyray.

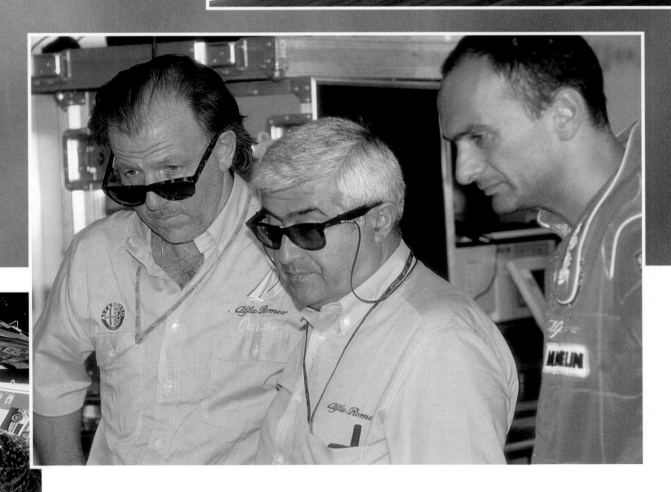

Clockwise from bottm left: The round 19 clash between Cleland and Rydell led to harsh words and protests (later withdrawn). The pit walkabout was massively popular. No points for Peugeot this time. A poor qualifying set-up cost Menu dear. Radisich pretends he's Tom Cruise - the Kiwi demonstrated a thundering NASCAR Ford Thunderbird

PHOTOGRAPHY: AUTOSPORT, BOTHWELL PHOTOGRAPHIC, ZOOOM

Will Hoy's victory in the first race of the day, after disposing of pole-sitter Rickard Rydell and early leader John Cleland at Druids on the opening lap, plus his second-place in the second race were good news for the 1991 champion. They were also the most straightforward things to come out of a day tarnished by protest and counter-protest.

Matt Neal takes two more Total Cup wins and moves inexorably to the privateers' title. His Ford Mondeo is actually a match for the works cars in race trim at Brands.

`In the first race, Rickard and John were fighting among themselves and I just took the outside line,' recalled a jubilant Hoy, `but even without that bit of help when they clashed, I'd still have won.'

That clash between Rydell's Volvo and Cleland's Vauxhall on the opening lap seemed just another BTCC incident at the time, albeit one that allowed Rydell to ultimately take back second from Cleland. Afterwards, though, it did take on extra significance.

In the second race, Rydell made an excellent start - `I'll do them all like that from now on' - and took the lead,

closely followed by Cleland.

To begin with, the Swede eked out the gap to something like two seconds. But it wasn't long before Cleland started to reel him in. By half-distance, the Vauxhall was breathing down the Volvo's neck. Then, going into Clearways for the 15th time, Rydell was slewing sideways - but did he fall, or was he pushed - and Cleland was through into the

BMW has another competitive showing, with Johnny Cecotto able to cling onto the lead group en route to fifth in race one.

Charlie Cox makes his racing return, just three months after the Thruxton accident that nearly killed him. Cox brings the first five-door Ford Mondeo to the BTCC.

lead, with Hoy taking the opportunity to sneak through into second.

Rydell was down into third and, had it not been for clutch problems for Gabriele Tarquini's fourth-placed Alfa, that might even have been one place lower.

Afterwards, the accusations began to fly. Both Cleland and Rydell were endorsed for their parts in each inci-

South African Touring Car Champion Mike Briggs steps into the Vauxhall berth left open by James Thompson's testing accident in Scotland. Briggs finishes sixth and fifth and will stand in for the injured Thompson for the rest of the season.

dent - normal stuff for the BTCC, one has to say - with Cleland adamant contact had not been made in the second of the two.

Both teams wanted more, however, saying that the incidents could both have affected the outcome of the championship. Volvo protested points leader Cleland's endorsement in race two, saying the punishment should be more severe - like a time penalty, for instance - while Vauxhall tit-for-tatted by asking for a more severe punishment to be bestowed on title runner-up Rydell for the first race barney.

It was all extremely messy and a rather sad and sordid way for the championship to reach its climax. And with the appeals not due to be heard until Snetterton in a fortnight, it was an unsatisfactory end to the weekend however you looked at it.

Touring car year 95-96

Brands Hatch
Round 18 - 30 Laps

1	W Hoy	Renault
2	R Rydell	Volvo
3	J Cleland	Vauxhall
4	A Menu	Renault
5	J Cecotto	BMW
6	M Briggs	Vauxhall
7	T Harvey	Volvo
8	D Warwick	Alfa Romeo
9	J Bailey	Toyota
10	J Kaye	Honda

Fastest Lap: R Rydell
Total Cup: M Neal

Round 14 - 15 Laps

1	J Cleland	Vauxhall
2	W Hoy	Renault
3	R Rydell	Volvo
4	G Tarquini	Alfa Romeo
5	M Briggs	Vauxhall
6	P Watts	Peugeot
7	T Harvey	Volvo
8	J Kaye	Honda
9	T Sugden	Toyota
10	D Leslie	Honda

Fastest Lap: J Cleland
Total Cup: M Neal

PHOTOGRAPHY: BOTHWELL

They trust Mobil ⓵
So can you

The Vauxhall Cavalier Touring cars are smothered with attention. It's hardly surprising when you see what they're put through.

And the experts at Vauxhall choose Mobil 1 to protect the inside of their powerful fuel injected engines.

They appreciate that fully synthetic

Mobil1, is the world's most advanced engine oil.

They know that Mobil 1 will ensure they get the maximum performance from their race engines while providing protection through the tough races ahead.

So whatever Vauxhall you drive, trust Mobil 1 from the start.

For information call FREE on 0800 585 995 (Mobil) and 0800 444 200 (Vauxhall)

BEHOLD THE ALFA 155. SALOON IT MAY BE, SEDATE IT'S NOT. IT'S AVAILABLE WITH OUR 150 BHP 2.0 T.SPARK 16V ENGINE, AS WELL AS THE 1.8 T.SPARK AND 2.5 V6. THE ENGINE COMBINES PERFECT BALANCE WITH TRUE ALFA ROMEO PERFORMANCE. YOU'D EXPECT NO LESS FROM THE ENGINEERS WHO'VE BUILT SOME OF THE WORLD'S FINEST RACING ENGINES. THIS 155 HANDLES EVEN BETTER THAN ITS PREDECESSOR. IT SITS

THE ALFA 155
AS SEEN BY OTHER ROAD USERS.

Cuore Sportivo

15MM LOWER AND HAS 26MM WIDER TRACK, GIVING IT ENHANCED SAFETY AND PIN-POINT PRECISION WHEN CHANGING LANES. DRIVER'S AIRBAG, ABS, SIDE IMPACT BARS, ELECTRONIC IMMOBILISER AND POWER STEERING ARE STANDARD, AS IS A 3 YEAR ALFA CARE DEALER WARRANTY. TRY IT AT YOUR LOCAL ALFA ROMEO DEALER OR PHONE 0800 718 000.

DEALER
3-YEAR
ALFACARE
WARRANTY

Burt's slick choice

Race one at Snetterton gave Kelvin Burt his first overall BTCC victory. Race two virtually decided the outcome of the title

Clockwise from above:
The BTCC circus fills the Snetterton paddock to capacity. Radisich (left) maybe
smiling, but he was outscored by Mondeo
privateers Gravett (right) and and Neal. A
Brilliant drive from the back on slicks
brought second place for Patrick Watts.
Burt heads for a great win in race one. Tim
Harvey's Volvo bashes
Alain Menu out of the
drivers' title chase

PHOTOGRAPHY: AUTOSPORT, BOTHWELL PHOTOGRAPHIC, ZOOM, IAN HARRISON, BRYN WILLIAMS

Snetterton
Rounds 20 & 21

Clockwise from bottom left: Kelvin Burt hoists the trophy after his race one triumph. David Leslie and the Honda were second on the road in race one. Cecotto set fastest lap in race one after a stop to fit slicks. Rydell parked in a bush after backing past an ambulance - his title hopes dived

PHOTOGRAPHY: AUTOSPORT, BOTHWELL PHOTOGRAPHIC, ZOOM,

Clockwise from bottom left: Will Hoy was back on the winners' step of the podium after a fine run in race two. Alain Menu got Volvo'd - twice by Tim Harvey. Mike Briggs was heading for the podium in race one before he clashed with David Leslie. Julian Bailey - sixth for Toyota. David Leslie lost second place because of his part in Briggs's off

Rain just minutes before the start of race one at a cold and windy Snetterton caused a tyre conundrum - wet, slick, or intermediate. Those who chose wets paid dearly as the track dried in the later laps. But those who'd gambled, including Ford's Kelvin Burt, reaped the benefits.

Rickard Rydell's Volvo, John Cleland's Vauxhall, the Renault of Alain Menu and Tim Harvey's Volvo - all wet-shod - made the early running. But it wasn't too long before Harvey was in trouble

Johnny Cecotto scored a point for BMW in race one, despite making a pit stop to change from wets to slicks. The Venezuelan also took the fastest lap of the race.

Burt duly took the chequered flag, noting how `I'd put the intermediates on with roughly 30s to go and then had to take it easy in the opening laps before things really dried out.' But Leslie found his second for Honda a short-lived affair, following

and Cleland held third, fourth and fifth. But at Sear for the first time, Harvey and Menu made contact, dropping the Renault to the back of the field and putting Harvey in third behind Hoy. Again, the whole incident was surrounded in controversy.

At the front, Rydell continued to lead until lap 15 until, without warning, the Volvo was off the track at Riches and heading for an emergency vehicle gap. Luckily the Volvo missed everything solid, but it was a tragic blow for the Swede's title chances.

`I suddenly had the brake pedal go long,' recalled Rydell, `and I tried to straightline it, but I just couldn't hold it.'

That handed Hoy his second victory in as many races, with Harvey finishing second and Cleland taking more valuable points for third, ahead of best privateer Matt Neal's Mondeo. Mathematically, clinching the title was on for Cleland at the very next round, Oulton Park.

Robb Gravett's record-breaking privateer podium finish gave him the Total Cup victory in race one, but Matt Neal's fourth overall and Total Cup win in race two made the Midlander's landing of the £25,000 first prize a virtual formality at Oulton Park.

after straight-lining the Russell chicane and then going off at Sear and taking menu with him.

As the track dried, the likes of Burt, Mike Briggs' Vauxhall and David Leslie's Honda began to make their moves, thanks to choosing intermediates or cut slicks.

With only a couple of laps to go, Burt was romping away in a lead he'd taken on lap nine, with Briggs second and Leslie third. However, a controversial coming together between Leslie and Briggs at the Esses for the last time saw Briggs down to eighth, Leslie second and Watts' Peugeot, which had started right at the very back of the grid, an incredible third.

the imposition of a 10s penalty. That put Watts into Peugeot's best finish of the season and took privateer Robb Gravett into a sensational third overall.

Despite finishing 13th on the road, points leader Cleland was satisfied due to Rydell, his only real challenger, finishing 14th. `It's the first time I've ever felt happy at being 13th,' chuckled the Scot.

Race two was run in dry conditions from the off. Rydell took the lead as Menu bogged down slightly, while Harvey, Will Hoy's Renault

Rickard Rydell takes poles number 12 and 13, giving him a staggering hit rate of 62%.

Both Vauxhall and Volvo dropped their appeals lodged at Brands in the week prior to Snetterton.

Honda took its case to an RAC tribunal following the rejection of its appeal against David Leslie's 10s penalty for the incident with Mike Briggs' Vauxhall. Leslie's second on the road would have been Honda's best finish since entering the BTCC.

PHOTOGRAPHY: BOTHWELL, MICK WALKER

Touring car year 95-96

Snetterton
Round 20 - 18 Laps

1	K Burt	Ford
2	P Watts	Peugeot
3	R Gravett	Ford
4	G Tarquini	Alfa Romeo
5	R Kaye	Ford
6	T Sugden	Toyota
7	M Briggs	Vauxhall
8	D Leslie	Honda
9	P Radisich	Ford
10	J Cecotto	BMW

Fastest Lap: J Cecotto
Total Cup: R Gravett

Round 21 - 20 Laps

1	W Hoy	Renault
2	T Harvey	Volvo
3	J Cleland	Vauxhall
4	M Neal	Ford
5	M Briggs	Vauxhall
6	J Bailey	Toyota
7	T Sugden	Toyota
8	D Leslie	Honda
9	J Kaye	Honda
10	A Menu	Renault

Fastest Lap: R Rydell
Total Cup: M Neal

Valvoline

TEAM Mondeo

VALVOLINE®

"In more than 100 countries
People who know use Valvoline Motor Oil"

We race. You get the result.

John, King of the Scots

John Cleland took his second BTCC title with two races to spare. But two wins for Renault's Alain Menu meant the race for the manufacturers' award would go down to the wire

Clockwise from below:
Gabriele Tarquini was a competitive fourth in race one. Tim Sugden didn't complete a single racing lap after a pair of shunts. The new champion chats with team mate Mike Briggs. Julian Bailey spun after the power-steering failed

Oulton Park
Rounds *22 & 23*

Clockwise from right:

Alain Menu dominated on the Fosters circuit to take two wins. Matt Neal clinched the Total Cup with two wins. Cecotto and Brabham worked hard for BMW. David Leslie achieved the coveted podium slot for Honda. Menu and Williams Renault team director Ian Harrison - wishing the winning streak had started earlier?

PHOTOGRAPHY: AUTOSPORT, BOTHWELL PHOTOGRAPHIC

PHOTOGRAPHY: AUTOSPORT, BOTHWELL, BRYN WILLIAMS, ALLSPORT

Oulton Park
Rounds 22 & 23

Clockwise from below: Cleland and Hoy share a joke. Cleland and the Cavalier - the most consistently competitive combination this year. It was mighty crowded at Fosters on lap one. Bailey's new-evo Carina was quick. Matt Neal with the other privateers behind

John Cleland came to Oulton Park with a 52-point lead over Volvo's Rickard Rydell and only 96 points available from the final four races. And with 48 on offer at Oulton, Rydell had to at least outscore the Vauxhall man by four. Alain Menu could also take the title, but such were the mathematics of such a thing that he was virtually ruled out from the start - not because of what he would need to do, but because of what others would need not to do.

After practice, things already looked to be slipping away from Rydell. Menu was on pole twice, Cleland was second twice... and the Swede was sixth and 18th, with the second session time coming after the team fitted two fifth gears by mistake. Not a good start.

With the smaller Fosters circuit in BTCC use for the first time, and the tight Fosters corner which leads back onto the full circuit coming in for a lot of criticism for its tightness, many expected first lap chaos. They didn't get it. Instead, Cleland dived into the lead at the start of race one, but was overhauled by Menu at Lodge at the end of the lap.

`John had the championship on his mind,' said the Swiss, `so I knew it would be silly for him to try anything on.'

Will Hoy took second from Cleland at Lodge on lap five, making it a Renault one-two. But that was basically that. Gabriele Tarquini took another strong fourth for Alfa after Julian Bailey's seemingly podium-bound Toyota went out with power steering failure and Rickard Rydell came in fifth, with his championship hopes beginning to come crashing around his ears.

Race two was more of the same, except that his time Menu led from the start and was able to resume control of the race following the first appearance of the BTCC's new safety car.

`John gave me a little trouble before the safety car came out,' said Menu afterwards, `but afterwards, I was able to pull away quite easily and made sure I had a good gap.'

Cleland held second to the flag, but not without a couple of big moments as it began to rain in the closing laps, and also having to put up with some considerable pressure from David

Menu's double victory puts Renault to within seven points of Vauxhall in the manufacturers' title chase and elevates the Swiss to second in the drivers' battle, above the unfortunate Rickard Rydell.

Accidents to Toyota's Tim Sugden on the opening laps of each race mean the Yorkshireman completes less than half a racing lap all weekend.

Leslie's Honda, which annexed its second on-the-road podium in consecutive races - but the first allowed to stand.

`I've got to be pleased with that,' said Leslie, `but I still wish that John's big moment had lasted just a little big longer.'

Rydell had managed to scramble his way to 10th, but that was way, way short of what was required to keep the title fight alive until the final round.

`We lost our championship before today,' mused the disappointed Swede, `but we will come back next year and we will win then.'

Cleland was jubilant, having captured 2-litre touring car racing's glittering prize. `Not bad for an old-timer in an old fleet car, eh?' grinned the 43-year-old, before adding that `to win in 1989 was great, but now this is the world's toughest 2-litre touring car series, so this is a real honour.'

Matt Neal clinches the Total Cup in the best way possible - winning both races. Neal's only remaining challenger, Richard Kaye, has to be content with two thirds in class, ending his chances, but also bringing his runner-up spot under pressure from Nigel Smith with two races to go.

Touring car year 95-96

Oulton Park
Round 22 - 22 Laps

1	A Menu	Renault
2	W Hoy	Renault
3	J Cleland	Vauxhall
4	G Tarquini	Alfa Romeo
5	R Rydell	Volvo
6	D Leslie	Honda
7	J Kaye	Honda
8	D Warwick	Alfa Romeo
9	S Harrison	Peugeot
10	K Burt	Ford

Fastest Lap: Menu
Total Cup: M Neal

Round 23 - 24 Laps

1	A Menu	Renault
2	J Cleland	Vauxhall
3	D Leslie	Honda
4	J Bailey	Toyota
5	T Harvey	Volvo
6	J Cecotto	BMW
7	K Burt	Ford
8	M Briggs	Vauxhall
9	J Kaye	Honda
10	R Rydell	Volvo

Fastest Lap: A Menu
Total Cup: M Neal

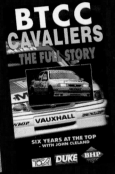

PHOTOGRAPHY: AUTOSPORT, JED LEICESTER, BRYN WILLIAMS, DEAN POWELL

Silverstone
Rounds 24 & 25

Clockwise from top right:
The Williams Renault Dealer Racing crew celebrates its manufacturers' title. Briggs, Cecotto, Brabham, Burt and Radisich (right to left). Hoy's bumper flies over Cleland and Bailey. Sad end to privateer Nigel Smith's season. Pits activity reflected in the side window of Hoy's winning Renault Laguna

Renault takes its glory

A win apiece for Alain Menu and Will Hoy gave Renault the manufacturers' title and ensured that Vauxhall didn't take all the trophies

Silverstone
Rounds 24 & 25

Clockwise from bottom:
Hoy heads for his third win of the season. Cleland flies the St Andrew's cross. Menu battles with Leslie during race two. The weather wasn't kind to the flag wavers. Hoy and daughter answer Cleland's incisive questions. A trip over the Copse kerbing left Bailey's Carina sparking merrily.

PHOTOGRAPHY: AUTOSPORT, JED LEICESTER, SIMON HILDREW, JACKIE DANE, COLIN MCMASTER

Alain Menu's double victory at Oulton Park had set up the sting. But it was a win apiece for the Swiss and his team mate Will Hoy which finally stole the BTCC manufacturers' title from under the nose of Vauxhall at the last gasp.

Pole position in race one for newly-crowned champion John Cleland aside, Renault completely dominated events at Silverstone, with Menu taking pole for the second race, plus both fastest laps, and Hoy and Menu dutifully following their team mate home in both races to end Williams Touring Car Engineering's first season with a pair of one-two results.

But at this point in the season, Cleland was beyond caring. The BTCC crown was his, and that's all that mattered.

Both races saw the BTCC introduce its new toy, the safety car, once again. And in each case, its deployment merely played further into the hands of Renault.

In race one, with pole-sitter Cleland having made his `worst start of the season', the Renault pair were already running one-two on the road when the safety car was brought into action after four laps of racing to allow Nigel Smith's stricken Cavalier to be pulled from the gravel.

At the restart, Menu blasted away into the lead, while Hoy held the pack up a little, prior to crossing the start-finish line. `I had a bit of a misfire at the restart,' quipped Hoy. Despite being well wide of the spirit of the rules, such a move was perfectly legal, and Menu was able to capitalise and record a comfortable victory.

Behind Hoy and Cleland, Kelvin Burt's Ford came in fourth, ahead of David Leslie's Honda and Mike Briggs' Vauxhall. A quick glance at the points revealed that that put Renault just one point behind Vauxhall in the manufacturers'.

Peugeot rookie Simon Harrison ends his season with a 100mph-plus crash that sees his 405 assaulting the wall out of Woodcote.

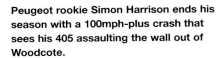

David Leslie's Honda is fastest in pre-race testing and lines up fifth and third on the grid.

🏁

Julian Bailey's Toyota again looks a potential podium contender, but is thwarted by a hanging front undertray.

Richard Kaye annexes second in the final Total Cup standings with a win and a second. Matt Neal rounds off his season with his 14th class win of the year in the final race.

The result also consolidated Menu's second in the points, as Rickard Rydell and Volvo once again suffered from the loss of form - and luck - that had blighted the Swedish combo's run-in to the end of the season.

For Cleland, a pair of thirds didn't allow him to equal Gabriele Tarquini's 1994 record of eight victories in a season. Indeed, Menu's win put him onto seven - one more than the title-winning Scot.

Race two saw Hoy take the lead, ahead of Menu, with Leslie holding third and Cleland fourth. And with Vauxhall needing to stay ahead of Renault to hang onto the manufacturers' lead, things were looking good for the Regie.

Cue the safety car again, this time to remove David Brabham's stranded BMW, and Renault was ready to play its two-car trick again. Sure enough, when the lights went off, Menu stayed back and Hoy exploded into an increased lead. `I had fallen asleep a little when they switched the safety car's lights off,' shrugged an unconvincing Menu.

Leslie began to put pressure on Menu and took the second spot. But it proved a temporary glitch in the Renault domination, with Menu out-dragging the Honda for the spot again a handful of laps later.

Leslie then found himself with Cleland breathing down his neck and desperate to make up ground in his forlorn struggle to get on terms with the Renaults. The Scots did finally swap places, but by then, it was all over bar the shouting - Renault had it in the bag, Hoy had his third victory of the season and Vauxhall had to be content with `just' the drivers' and teams' crowns.

Silverstone
Round 24 - 28 Laps

1	A Menu	Renault
2	W Hoy	Renault
3	J Cleland	Vauxhall
4	K Burt	Ford
5	D Leslie	Honda
6	M Briggs	Vauxhall
7	R Rydell	Volvo
8	D Warwick	Alfa Romeo
9	D Brabham	BMW
10	T Harvey	Volvo

Fastest Lap: A Menu
Total Cup: R Kaye

Round 25 - 28 Laps

1	W Hoy	Renault
2	A Menu	Renault
3	J Cleland	Vauxhall
4	D Leslie	Honda
5	J Bailey	Toyota
6	T Sudgen	Toyota
7	T Harvey	Volvo
8	P Watts	Peugeot
9	J Kaye	Honda
10	D Warwick	Alfa Romeo

Fastest Lap: A Menu
Total Cup: M Neal

Statistics

RACE VICTORIES

Drivers		Manufacturers	
1 Menu	7	1 Renault	10
2 Cleland	6	2 Vauxhall	7
3 Rydell	4	3 Volvo	6
4 Hoy	3	4 Ford	2
5 Harvey	2		
6 Thompson	1		
= Radisich	1		
= Burt	1		

POLE POSITIONS

Drivers		Manufacturers	
1 Rydell	13	1 Volvo	13
2 Menu	6	2 Vauxhall	6
3 Cleland	4	= Renault	6
4 Thompson	2		

FASTEST LAPS

Drivers		Manufacturers	
1 Menu	8	1 Renault	8
2 Cleland	5	2 Vauxhall	6
3 Rydell	4	3 Volvo	5
4 Radisich	3	4 Ford	4
5 Burt	1	5 Toyota	1
= Bailey	1	= BMW	1
= Thompson	1		
= Harvey	1		
= Cecotto	1		

MOST LAPS LED

Drivers		Manufacturers	
1 Menu	162	1 Renault	223
2 Cleland	95	2 Volvo	133
3 Rydell	90	3 Vauxhall	112
4 Hoy	61	4 Ford	56
5 Radisich	46		
6 Harvey	43		
7 Thompson	17		
8 Burt	10		

MOST TOP TEN FINISHES

Drivers		Manufacturers	
1 Cleland	22	1 Vauxhall	40
2 Menu	20	2 Volvo	38
3 Rydell	19	3 Renault	35
= Harvey	19	4 Toyota	29
5 Bailey	17	5 Ford	25
6 Hoy	15	6 Honda	24
7 Leslie	13	7 BMW	20
= Burt	13	8 Alfa Romeo	19
9 Sugden	12	9 Peugeot	14
= Radisich	12	10 Total Cup	6
11 Thompson	11		
= J Kaye	11		
etc.			

Wing Power

Important new Super Touring aerodynamic rules for 1995 allowed a rear wing, and a purpose-designed front airdam with integral splitter

Each manufacturer was required to lodge the specification of these devices with the FIA before the season began, and no changes were then permitted. This factor created difficulties for those manufacturers homologating cars for several national championships, featuring widely different circuit characteristics. It may go towards explaining, for example, why Alfa Romeo was less competitive in Britain in 1995.

A splitter is used to control the airflow to create downforce. A front-drive car is inherently prone to understeer, so front-end downforce is of great importance, increasing the grip of the front tyres. Furthermore,

downforce created on the underside of a car carries a relatively small aerodynamic drag penalty.

Generation of downforce in this area is the function not only of the splitter, but also an undertray extending under the nose to a point level with the front axle line. The length of the undertray, its height above the ground and its angle relative to the road (rake) are crucial influences on the downforce that can be generated.

Although the length of the undertray is restricted, it is important to keep the remainder of the underside as flat and clear of obstruction as possible, thus reducing turbulence, and therefore drag. The

ideal solution would be not permitted, so a team relies on careful design, including the location of silencers and fuel cells. However, most passenger cars have a step in the floorpan beneath the rear seats, a fuel tank protruding into the floorpan, and a bumper hanging down at the rear. On the Super Touring racecar, these must be all standard parts, so they handicap the racing aerodynamicists.

A primary function of the rearwing is to balance the car in high-speed corners where the splitter generates sufficient downforce to induce oversteer. An effective aerofoil requires free flow to both upper and lower surfaces, so those in Super Touring cannot truly be described as

The Cars

ALFA ROMEO 155 ts - Engine: 4 cylinder in line transverse mounted double overhead camshafts 16 valves Capacity: 1998cc Gearbox: 6 speed front-wheel drive L: 4487mm W: 1730mm H: 1410mm Wb: 2540mm Weight: 975kg F Susp: MacPherson struts R Susp: Trailing links Wheels: 8 in x 19 in

BMW 318i - Engine: 4 cylinder in line longitudinally mounted double overhead camshafts 16 valves Capacity: 1998cc Power: 275 bhp Gearbox: 6 speed rear-wheel drive L: 4433mm W: 1698mm H: 1270mm Wb: 2700mm Weight: 1025/1000kg F Susp: MacPherson struts R Susp: Central arm longitudinal double-track control arms Wheels: 8 in x 19 in

FORD MONDEO - Engine: 6 cylinder vee transverse mounted double overhead camshafts 24 valves Capacity: 1998cc Gearbox: 6 speed front-wheel drive L: 4481mm W: 1747mm H: 1372mm Wb: 2704mm Weight: 975kg F Susp: MacPherson struts R Susp: MacPherson struts Wheels: 8 in x 19 in

HONDA ACCORD - Engine: 4 cylinder in line transverse mounted double overhead camshafts 16 valves Capacity: 1998cc Gearbox: 6 speed front-wheel drive L: 4675mm W: 1715mm H: 1245mm Wb: 2720mm Weight: 975kg F Susp: Double wishbones R Susp: Double wishbones Wheels: 8.2 in x 18 in

PEUGEOT 405 Mi16 - Engine: 4 cylinder in line transverse mounted double overhead camshafts 16 valves Capacity: 1998cc Gearbox: 6 speed front-wheel drive L: 4410mm W: 1720mm H: 1360mm Wb: 2670mm Weight: 975kg F Susp: MacPherson struts R Susp: trailing arms Wheels: 8.3 in x 19 in

RENAULT LAGUNA - Engine: 4 cylinder in line transverse mounted double overhead camshafts 16 valves Capacity: 1998cc Power: 285bhp Gearbox: 6 speed front-wheel drive L: 4508mm W: 1752mm H: 1433mm Wb: 2670mm Weight: 975kg F Susp: MacPherson struts R Susp: Trailing arms Wheels: 8 in x 19 in

TOYOTA CARINA E - Engine: 4 cylinder in line transverse mounted double overhead camshafts 16 valves Capacity: 1998cc Power: 285bhp Gearbox: 6 speed front-wheel drive L: 4530mm W: 1695mm H: 1410mm Wb: 2580mm Weight: 975kg F Susp: MacPherson struts R Susp: MacPherson struts Wheels: 8 in x 19 in

VAUXHALL CAVALIER 16v - Engine: 4 cylinder in line transerve mounted double overhead camshafts 16 valves Capacity: 1998cc Power: 280bhp Gearbox: 6 speed front-wheel drive L: 4430mm W: 1700mm H: 1400mm Wb: 2600mm Weight: 975kg F Susp: MacPherson struts R Susp: Semi trailing arms Wheels: 8 in x 19 in

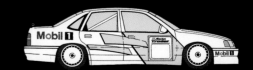

VOLVO 850 - Engine: 5 cylinder in line transverse mounted double overhead camshafts 20 valves Capacity: 1999cc Gearbox: 6 speed front-wheel drive L: 4670mm W: 1760mm H: 1430mm Wb: 2670mm Weight: 975kg F Susp: MacPherson struts R Susp: Trailing arms Wheels: 8.2 in x 19 in

wings. The rear wing is located just above the bootlid and directly behind the cabin superstructure. Even in free flow, it is too close to the bootlid surface to operate without interference, and the obstruction of the cabin can only exacerbate the problem.

The rear wing of the Williams Renault Laguna is noteworthly in this regard; with its tall, vertical, rear flap, it will act as a spoiler, rather than a conventional wing. A vertical surface at the rearmost point of the body is a simple way of generating downforce, by means of the high-pressure area it creates ahead of itself. In the case of a touring car, this downforce might also

be free of additional drag, because it is in the 'shadow' of the cabin.

To keep the driven wheels in contact with the track, it is important not to allow the car to pitch too much. This implies control of the attitude of the underside – a crucial consideration in all forms of track racing in exploiting ground-effect. In many motorsports classes, this control is achieved by severely restricting suspension movement, and the 1995 Super Touring cars used stiffer springs than their 1994 counterparts.

At 125mph (200kph), a standard road car may generate 80kg of 'lift' - a phenomenon which occurs when air passes over the pressure reduction.

Until 1995, Super Touring aerodynamic aids served only to reduce this effect. While the 1994 aerodynamic components had to be derived from parts in use on road cars, however, there was no minimum production requirement in 1995, so the latest aerodynamic aids were purpose-made and more efficient. The cars now generate measurable download, rather than just reducing lift. At present, the maximum downforce generated is about 135kg at the maximum speed of 160mph (260kph). At least 60% of the downforce acts on the front wheels. The typical downforce generated at 125mph (200kph) equContrary to

Super Touring cars are hi-tech under the surface, but still require traditional pit equipment and team work to win races

popular belief, the 2.0 litre Super Touring car does not have a tuned production engine. It has to retain a production block and head but the guts can be ripped out, to be replaced by bespoke racing parts. Even the bore and stroke can be changed at will. The four cylinder, 16 valve Vauxhall Super Touring engine has an 88mm bore compared to 84mm for a production unit.

Power Braking

Super Tourers don't stop as quickly as Formula One cars. That is because they don't have the same hi-tech carbonfibre brakes, right? Wrong!

Over the summer Williams tested a Formula One car with the same type of brakes as used on its Renault Laguna Super Tourer: Performance Friction Carbon Metallic PFC93 pads gripping traditional cast iron discs. Damon Hill was marginally quicker with these metal brakes, finding a slight advantage into certain corners.

Independent brake dynomometer tests confirm that the Super Touring brake attains a fractionally higher co-efficient of friction than a Formula One brake. The Super Tourer takes longer to stop from the same speed because it is almost twice as heavy as the Formula One car and because it has a lot less grip. It has a lot less grip because it has narrower tyres and a lot less downforce.

Last season the majority of Super Tourers generated lift rather than downforce. The advent of aerodynamic aids means that a car like the Laguna attains perhaps 90Kg downforce at 120mph compared to something like 900Kg for the Williams Renault FW17 at the same speed. But that humble 90Kg is not insignificant. This season Super Touring cars are braking significantly later.

The downforce falls off rapidly as speed reduces in the braking zone. The relationship between speed and downforce is such that downforce is slashed to a quarter of its value as speed is halved from 120mph to 60mph. Nevertheless, Super Touring drivers report that they feel the effect of downforce more in slow corners than in fast ones. This is explained by the fact that downforce has calmed the cars down, keeping them far more stable, particularly under braking and thus keeping tyre temperatures within the range at which optimum grip is produced.

Downforce has permitted Super Touring cars to exploit more of the formidable potential of their brakes, which are similar to those fitted to 240mph Le Mans Sports Prototypes a few years ago. Front drive cars still have far bigger brakes at the front than at the rear but this year, more stable, they are getting more work out of the rears, to the benefit of overall braking performance.

Still, however, the rear brakes tend to be thin, unventilated cast iron discs of 10.5" diameter worked by two piston calipers. Only the best front drive cars can exploit the power of Performance Friction pads at the rear but they are almost universal at the front where they are typically fitted into four piston calipers to grab a thick internally ventilated cast iron disc that can be as large as 14.8" in diameter.

The state of the art in Super Touring front brakes is the water cooled AP four piston caliper fitted to the Williams Renault Laguna. The water flows through internal passageways and is pumped through an external radiator. It sucks heat out of the Carbon Metallic pads, improving their effectiveness. Nevertheless, for all the water cooling, ultra high power pads and downforce it still isn't possible for a front drive car to turn into a corner under the brakes without locking a front wheel. Thereby lies one advantage of rear drive...

Power Limit

Super Touring engine development continues to gain vital fractions of a second over every lap

John Cleland's British Championship winning engine was designed, developed and prepared by Swindon Racing Engines (SRE), as have been Vauxhall factory engines throughout the current formula. SRE produces engines for a number of motorsport categories and the prototype '95 Super Touring engine found its way into a 2.0 litre hillclimb car, producing 299.7bhp at 8,800rpm.

An engine's horsepower is the product of its torque multiplied by its crankshaft speed. In Super Touring a modest crankshaft speed limit of 8500rpm is imposed by the mandatory electronic rev limiter. At its maximum 8,500rpm Cleland's engine produces 296bhp. SRE could easily attain over 300bhp at the same engine speed but to do so it would have to sacrifice power at lower engine speeds, to the detriment of overall performance.

Interestingly, early in the development of the engine SRE ran a back to back track test of a 'high torque' 250bhp engine against a (then standard) 270bhp engine. The torque advantage was primarily at the low end of the engine speed range and data acquisition showed that it was not exploited on track. Nevertheless, SRE boss John Dunn reveals that both engines produced almost the same lap times.

'An engine that works well low down tends to work better. It somehow seems to know that it is better down there and responds to that! It must be to do with its transient performance. Certainly, that back to back test emphasised that maximum power is not as critical as everyone thinks: a lot of performance is in cornering and traction...' Nevertheless, each year the competition in Super Touring becomes hotter and nowadays even if an engine development is only worth fractions of a second it is worth pursuing. A few more top end horsepower are valuable, provided they don't come at the expense of performance lower down the scale. Last year's SRE Vauxhall engine produced 285bhp - a new camshaft with appropriate intake and exhaust tuning lifted the entire power curve a small but significant amount. Of course, the exercise wasn't as straightforward as it sounds and it wasn't without its drawbacks...

No pain no gain. This year's slight performance increase came at the cost of longevity. The aim was to flow more air, primarily by resort to a more radical camshaft providing, in the words of Dunn; 'A very high lift and a very high rate of acceleration of the valve off its seat - one that I wouldn't have even dreamt of using a couple of years ago!'

SRE designs its own camshafts and Dunn reports that last year valve lift was 440 thou inlet, 420 thou exhaust. The '95 figures are undisclosed but represent 'a significant increase over those!' The entire valve train - now 'very highly stressed' - had to be redesigned, with lighter valves, retainers and tappets and suitable springs.

Virtually every component in the valvetrain was redesigned for improved durability. Nevertheless, the engine will not stand as much abuse as before. The previous single valve spring seemed unbreakable but now far more highly stressed twin coils are the Achilles heel of the engine, even though 8500rpm is not particularly high by the operating speeds of contemporary race engines. Mechanical over-revs do not go much beyond 10,000rpm but Dunn points out that it is the instantaneous rate of acceleration that does the damage...

At the time of writing the engine had only suffered one spring failure on track, that during early testing and caused by a hidden imperfection in the spring wire. It is impossible to ensure that all springs are perfect and it is primarily to guard against the danger of spring failure that engine rebuilds are now every 500 miles whereas the '94 engine could run comfortably over 1000 miles. Such is the price of progress in one of the most fiercely contested of all motor racing arenas.ates to about 10% of vehicle weight. By comparison, an F1 car at the same speed would generate 200% of vehicle weight.

Braking efficiency is improved by the downforce acting on the tyres and, as a result, turn-in is better, which enables the driver to carry more speed through the corner. The cars are also easier on tyres, because the downforce improves grip, greatly reducing wheelspin and understeer.

Second generation touring cars such as Volvo, feature low line engine installations. The block and head are from production engines, in this case Alfa Romeo.

Differential Secrets

The fact that the majority of road cars are front wheel drive leads some people to assume that front drive is superior to rear drive for a front engined car. Consider that any one tyre can only do so much work - by asking the fronts to do all the work the front drive car is at an inherent disadvantage compared to the rear drive car which shares the work load more evenly. This disadvantage is most apparent as the front drive car tries to brake into corners and to accelerate out of them - without running out of road at the exit.

Most Super Touring Cars are front drive. For both driver and engineer front drive is an unusual and taxing challenge. It demands an approach entirely different from that of the traditional racing car - and all involved in running front drive Super Touring cars are still learning. What has become clear is the central importance of the differential in optimising the performance of the car throughout the braking and cornering sequence.

There are two basics types of racing differential that are employed in Super Touring - the plate-type and the Viscous Coupling (VC). Both are sophisticated units that have to be set up correctly for maximum performance. In theory a spot-on plate-type is reckoned to be slightly superior to a VC but a VC is more tolerant and is often the more practical option given the ever changing factors - in particular track surface condition - that prevail during the rigours of a TOCA meeting.

There is no such thing as the ultimate differential. A VC tends to be preferable under braking when a plate-type can snatch and destabilise the car. On the other hand front drive Super Tourers tend to be able to get the power down earlier with a plate-type, which locks in response to transmitted torque rather than wheel speed differentials. This year Vauxhall ran a plate-type differential, Ford a VC. Volvo and Renault had some more ambitious developments.

Mirroring development in Formula One (TWR has links with Ligier as well as Volvo, Williams runs the Renault), Super Touring cars have been equipped with electronically controlled differentials. In fact the concept was pioneered by Alfa Romeo in 1994; TWR and Williams have been developing more sophisticated versions.

The concept is that the all important characteristics of the differential are controlled by an electro-hydraulic system. For some time now four wheel drive rally cars have been equipped with 'active' centre differentials, the electronic control system automatically reacting to appropriate sensor inputs. This would not be legal for Formula One or Super Touring but the '95 regulations for both categories permitted the use of electro-hydraulic control, provided that the characteristics were fixed by some form of switch (open rather than closed loop control).

Thus, in the case of the electronically controlled differentials developed for Super Touring, the characteristics were controlled by a switch on the dash board. The driver was at liberty to alter the characteristics by a flick of the switch at any time - even in mid corner if that conferred an advantage. In some instances it did.

It is possible that this avenue of development was actually more advanced in Super Touring than in Formula One this past year, given the greater relative importance of differential characteristics with front drive and extremely limited downforce.

Clockwise from bottom right:
The 39-car field sets off for the second leg. Frank Biela and Audi were dominant. Alain Menu put in the best run of the BTCC boys - fifth in leg two. Biela (centre), Yvan Muller (right) and Steve Soper celebrate after leg one. The 'school' photo - 39 drivers from 15 countries

Audi Biela crush demo

Audi shook the BTCC brigade with its domination of the international showdown. Frank Biela won from team mate Emanuele Pirro and BMW's Steve Soper. Next year the A4 is BTCC-bound

1/2 April
QUALIFYING

	ROUND 1			ROUND 2	
1	Rickard RYDELL	1:38.50	1	Rickard RYDELL	1:38.71
2	John CLELAND	1:38.65	2	Alain MENU	1:39.41
3	Alain MENU	1:38.77	3	James THOMPSON	1:39.48
4	Paul RADISICH	1:38.78	4	Paul RADISICH	1:39.56
5	Tim HARVEY	1:39.11	5	Tim HARVEY	1:39.57
6	Johnny CECOTTO	1:39.23	6	John CLELAND	1:39.76
7	James THOMPSON	1:39.23	7	Johnny CECOTTO	1:39.86
8	Tim SUGDEN	1:39.54	8	Julian BAILEY	1:39.88
9	David LESLIE	1:39.64	9	Will HOY	1:39.90
10	Julian BAILEY	1:39.65	10	Simon HARRISON	1:39.93
11	Will HOY	1:39.84	11	Tim SUGDEN	1:40.01
12	Patrick WATTS	1:39.86	12	Giampiero SIMONI	1:40.11
13	Giampiero SIMONI	1:39.94	13	David LESLIE	1:40.15
14	Kelvin BURT	1:39.94	14	Patrick WATTS	1:40.18
15	David BRABHAM	1:40.06	15	Kelvin BURT	1:40.21
16	Simon HARRISON	1:40.08	16	Matt NEAL	1:40.22
17	Derek WARWICK	1:40.20	17	James KAYE	1:40.50
18	Matt NEAL	1:40.35	18	David BRABHAM	1:40.53
19	James KAYE	1:40.39	19	Derek WARWICK	1:40.77
20	Richard KAYE	1:41.52	20	Charlie COX	1:40.88
21	Robb GRAVETT	1:43.33	21	Richard KAYE	1:42.38
22	Charlie COX	1:43.50	22	Robb GRAVETT	1:42.79
23	Nigel SMITH	2:02.46	23	Nigel SMITH	1:43.36
			24	Hamish IRVINE	1:47.28

RESULTS - ROUND 1
18 laps, 57.78 miles

			Time/laps	Best lap
1	John CLELAND	Vauxhall Cavalier 16V	30:30.49	1:40.30
2	Alain MENU	Renault Laguna	30:36.43	1:40.90
3	Paul RADISICH	Ford Mondeo Ghia	30:39.13	1:41.02
4	Rickard RYDELL	Volvo 850 20V	30:39.86	1:41.14
5	Johnny CECOTTO	BMW 318iS	30:40.63	1:40.82
6	Will HOY	Renault Laguna	30:43.87	1:40.56
7	James THOMPSON	Vauxhall Cavalier 16V	30:44.26	1:41.01
8	Tim HARVEY	Volvo 850 20V	30:44.63	1:40.91
9	Tim SUGDEN	Toyota Carina E	30:48.75	1:41.25
10	Giampiero SIMONI	Alfa Romeo 155	30:50.04	1:41.03

11 James KAYE (Honda Accord), 30:53.39; 12 David BRABHAM (BMW 318iS), 30:57.66; 13 Patrick WATTS (Peugeot 405), 30:59.11; 14 Simon HARRISON (Peugeot 405), 31:11.24; 15 Matt NEAL (Ford Mondeo Ghia), 31:14.33; 16 Nigel SMITH (Vauxhall Cavalier 16v), 31:19.62; 17 Richard KAYE (Ford Mondeo Ghia), 31:20.71; 18 Charlie COX (Ford Mondeo Ghia), 31:25.78; 19 Robb GRAVETT (Vauxhall Cavalier 16v), 31:30.30; **Retired:** Kelvin BURT (Ford Mondeo Ghia), 8 laps, clutch; Hamish IRVINE (Peugeot 405), 7 laps, engine; Derek WARWICK (Alfa Romeo 155), 6 laps, accident; Julian BAILEY (Toyota Carina E), 3 laps, accident; David LESLIE (Honda Accord), 2 laps, steering.

RESULTS - ROUND 2
18 laps, 57.78 miles

			Time/laps	Best lap
1	Rickard RYDELL	Volvo 850 20V	30:26.66	1:39.80
2	John CLELAND	Vauxhall Cavalier 16V	30:33.75	1:41.16
3	Tim HARVEY	Volvo 850 20V	30:35.69	1:41.06
4	Alain MENU	Renault Laguna	30:38.50	1:41.16
5	Will HOY	Renault Laguna	30:40.61	1:40.98
6	Paul RADISICH	Ford Mondeo Ghia	30:44.94	1:41.28
7	James THOMPSON	Vauxhall Cavalier 16V	30:46.44	1:40.86
8	Johnny CECOTTO	BMW 318i	30:49.11	1:41.21
9	Giampiero SIMONI	Alfa Romeo 155	30:51.59	1:41.74
10	James KAYE	Honda Accord	30:55.03	1:41.66

11 Patrick WATTS (Peugeot 405), 30:56.10; 12 David BRABHAM (BMW 318i), 30:56.49; 13 Kelvin BURT (Ford Mondeo Ghia), 31:03.87; 14 Matt NEAL (Ford Mondeo Ghia), 31:13.19; 15 Robb GRAVETT (Vauxhall Cavalier 16v), 31:20.09; 16 Nigel SMITH (Vauxhall Cavalier 16v), 32:15.20; 17 Simon HARRISON (Peugeot 405), 15 laps; 18 Hamish IRVINE (Peugeot 405), 13 laps; **Retired:** Charlie COX (Ford Mondeo Ghia), 15 laps, accident; Julian BAILEY (Toyota Carina E), 15 laps, accident; David LESLIE (Honda Accord), 10 laps, gearbox; Richard KAYE (Ford Mondeo Ghia), 9 laps, overheating; Tim SUGDEN (Toyota Carina E), 8 laps, engine; Derek WARWICK (Alfa

16/17 April
QUALIFYING

	ROUND 3			ROUND 4	
1	Rickard RYDELL	0:45.89	1	Rickard RYDELL	0:45.94
2	John CLELAND	0:46.07	2	James THOMPSON	0:46.08
3	James THOMPSON	0:46.10	3	John CLELAND	0:46.22
4	Tim HARVEY	0:46.10	4	Alain MENU	0:46.32
5	Alain MENU	0:46.23	5	Kelvin BURT	0:46.43
6	James KAYE	0:46.31	6	Tim HARVEY	0:46.50
7	Patrick WATTS	0:46.33	7	Tim SUGDEN	0:46.51
8	Tim SUGDEN	0:46.38	8	Johnny CECOTTO	0:46.55
9	Johnny CECOTTO	0:46.38	9	Simon HARRISON	0:46.58
10	Paul RADISICH	0:46.41	10	Patrick WATTS	0:46.59
11	Will HOY	0:46.41	11	Giampiero SIMONI	0:46.64
12	Julian BAILEY	0:46.46	12	Derek WARWICK	0:46.66
13	Simon HARRISON	0:46.51	13	Paul RADISICH	0:46.66
14	David BRABHAM	0:46.52	14	David BRABHAM	0:46.68
15	Derek WARWICK	0:46.61	15	Julian BAILEY	0:46.71
16	Kelvin BURT	0:46.69	16	Matt NEAL	0:47.01
17	Giampiero SIMONI	0:46.70	17	Richard KAYE	0:47.13
18	David LESLIE	0:46.91	18	Nigel SMITH	0:47.36
19	Richard KAYE	0:47.22	19	Charlie COX	0:47.55
20	Nigel SMITH	0:47.37	20	Hamish IRVINE	0:50.08
21	Charlie COX	0:47.37	21	Will HOY	0:50.19
22	Matt NEAL	0:47.38			
23	Hamish IRVINE	0:49.92			

RESULTS - ROUND 3
25 laps, 30.77 miles

			Time/laps	Best lap
1	Tim HARVEY	Volvo 850 20V	23:45.55	0:55.88
2	Paul RADISICH	Ford Mondeo Ghia	23:51.49	0:55.44
3	Kelvin BURT	Ford Mondeo Ghia	23:54.65	0:55.73
4	David BRABHAM	BMW 318i	24:05.17	0:56.08
5	Charlie COX	Ford Mondeo Ghia	24 laps	0:57.30
6	Julian BAILEY	Toyota Carina E	24 laps	0:57.58
7	Alain MENU	Renault Laguna	24 laps	0:57.24
8	Patrick WATTS	Peugeot 405	24 laps	0:57.46
9	Will HOY	Renault Laguna	24 laps	0:57.35
10	Giampiero SIMONI	Alfa Romeo 155	24 laps	0:57.57

11 Johnny CECOTTO (BMW 318i), 24 laps; 12 Derek WARWICK (Alfa Romeo 155), 24 laps; 13 Rickard RYDELL (Volvo 850 20V), 24 laps; 14 Tim SUGDEN (Toyota Carina E), 24 laps; 15 Simon HARRISON (Peugeot 405), 24 laps; 16 Matt NEAL (Ford Mondeo Ghia), 24 laps; 17 David LESLIE (Honda Accord), 24 laps; 18 Nigel SMITH (Vauxhall Cavalier 16v), 24 laps; 19 James KAYE (Honda Accord), 24 laps; 20 Richard KAYE (Ford Mondeo Ghia), 24 laps; James THOMPSON (Vauxhall Cavalier 16V), 24 laps; **Retired:** Hamish IRVINE (Peugeot 405), 4 laps, accident; John CLELAND (Vauxhall Cavalier 16V), 1 lap, accident.

RESULTS - ROUND 4
27 laps, 33.23 miles

			Time/laps	Best lap
1	Tim HARVEY	Volvo 850 20V	24:56.63	0:54.75
2	James THOMPSON	Vauxhall Cavalier 16V	24:58.32	0:54.53
3	Rickard RYDELL	Volvo 850 20V	25:01.21	0:54.66
4	Kelvin BURT	Ford Mondeo Ghia	25:02.09	0:54.15
5	Johnny CECOTTO	BMW 318i	25:03.79	0:54.36
6	David BRABHAM	BMW 318i	25:04.68	0:54.63
7	Will HOY	Renault Laguna	25:11.50	0:54.39
8	Julian BAILEY	Toyota Carina E	25:12.69	0:54.89
9	Alain MENU	Renault Laguna	25:14.66	0:54.73
10	Tim SUGDEN	Toyota Carina E	25:25.75	0:55.49

11 Simon HARRISON (Peugeot 405), 25:26.80; 12 Giampiero SIMONI (Alfa Romeo 155), 25:28.09; 13 Matt NEAL (Ford Mondeo Ghia), 25:28.50; 14 James KAYE (Honda Accord), 25:34.36; 15 Charlie COX (Ford Mondeo Ghia), 25:48.04; 16 Nigel SMITH (Vauxhall Cavalier 16v), 25:48.68; 17 David LESLIE (Honda Accord), 26 laps; 18 Hamish IRVINE (Peugeot 405), 24 laps; 19 Richard KAYE (Ford Mondeo Ghia), 16 laps; **Retired:** Derek WARWICK (Alfa Romeo 155), 1 lap, accident; John CLELAND (Vauxhall Cavalier 16V), 1 lap, accident.

UNISYS

6/8 May
QUALIFYING

	ROUND 5			ROUND 6	
1	Alain MENU	1:18.262	1	James THOMPSON	1:18.229
2	John CLELAND	1:18.334	2	Will HOY	1:18.246
3	Paul RADISICH	1:18.716	3	Alain MENU	1:18.258
4	James THOMPSON	1:18.811	4	Rickard RYDELL	1:18.269
5	Rickard RYDELL	1:18.833	5	John CLELAND	1:18.296
6	Tim HARVEY	1:18.861	6	Paul RADISICH	1:18.689
7	Kelvin BURT	1:19.076	7	Kelvin BURT	1:18.695
8	Matt NEAL	1:19.244	8	Patrick WATTS	1:18.927
9	Patrick WATTS	1:19.284	9	Simon HARRISON	1:19.082
10	Giampiero SIMONI	1:19.329	10	Matt NEAL	1:19.146
11	Will HOY	1:19.428	11	Tim SUGDEN	1:19.248
12	Johnny CECOTTO	1:19.516	12	Tim HARVEY	1:19.254
13	David BRABHAM	1:19.767	13	Johnny CECOTTO	1:19.355
14	Tim SUGDEN	1:19.964	14	David BRABHAM	1:19.480
15	Derek WARWICK	1:20.049	15	Giampiero SIMONI	1:19.511
16	James KAYE	1:20.366	16	Derek WARWICK	1:19.769
17	Simon HARRISON	1:20.435	17	James KAYE	1:19.847
18	David LESLIE	1:20.578	18	Julian BAILEY	1:19.875
19	Julian BAILEY	1:20.608	19	David LESLIE	1:21.003
20	Nigel SMITH	1:21.356	20	Charlie COX	1:21.029
21	Charlie COX	1:21.472	21	Nigel SMITH	1:21.032
22	Richard KAYE	1:22.840	22	Richard KAYE	1:21.679
23	Hamish IRVINE	1:25.446	23	Hamish IRVINE	1:25.177

RESULTS - ROUND 5
20 laps, 47.12 miles

			Time/laps	Best lap
1	Alain MENU	Renault Laguna	26:39.08	1:18.61
2	John CLELAND	Vauxhall Cavalier 16V	26:39.41	1:19.00
3	Patrick WATTS	Peugeot 405	27:05.25	1:19.77
4	Tim SUGDEN	Toyota Carina E	27:08.56	1:19.75
5	David BRABHAM	BMW 318iS	27:09.63	1:20.10
6	Giampiero SIMONI	Alfa Romeo 155	27:09.98	1:20.14
7	Julian BAILEY	Toyota Carina E	27:11.80	1:20.66
8	David LESLIE	Honda Accord	27:16.67	1:20.40
9	Rickard RYDELL	Volvo 850 20V	27:25.61	1:20.09
10	Simon HARRISON	Peugeot 405	27:26.41	1:20.64

11 Nigel SMITH (Vauxhall Cavalier 16v), 27:29.97; 12 Derek WARWICK (Alfa Romeo 155), 28:00.67; 13 Charlie COX (Ford Mondeo Ghia), 28:01.51; 14 Richard KAYE (Ford Mondeo Ghia), 28:04.03; 15 Tim HARVEY (Volvo 850 20V), 19 laps; 16 James KAYE (Honda Accord), 18 laps; **Retired:** James THOMPSON (Vauxhall Cavalier 16V), 15 laps, tyre; Hamish IRVINE (Peugeot 405), 14 laps, engine; Johnny CECOTTO (BMW 318iS), 10 laps, tyres; Kelvin BURT (Ford Mondeo Ghia), 9 laps, accident; Paul RADISICH (Ford Mondeo Ghia), 7 laps, steering; Will HOY (Renault Laguna), 6 laps, steering; Matt NEAL (Ford Mondeo Ghia), 2 laps, accident.

RESULTS - ROUND 6
17 laps, 40.05 miles

			Time/laps	Best lap
1	James THOMPSON	Vauxhall Cavalier 16V	22:38.48	1:18.84
2	Alain MENU	Renault Laguna	22:41.33	1:19.10
3	Kelvin BURT	Ford Mondeo Ghia	22:45.38	1:19.48
4	Rickard RYDELL	Volvo 850 20V	22:45.57	1:19.10
5	John CLELAND	Vauxhall Cavalier 16V	22:52.16	1:19.13
6	Paul RADISICH	Ford Mondeo Ghia	22:53.38	1:19.20
7	Tim HARVEY	Volvo 850 20V	22:55.33	1:19.03
8	Julian BAILEY	Toyota Carina E	22:55.65	1:19.61
9	Simon HARRISON	Peugeot 405	22:58.12	1:19.34
10	Giampiero SIMONI	Alfa Romeo 155	22:59.62	1:19.80

11 Johnny CECOTTO (BMW 318iS), 23:03.10; 12 David LESLIE (Honda Accord), 23:08.53; 13 James KAYE (Honda Accord), 23:09.60; 14 Nigel SMITH (Vauxhall Cavalier 16v), 23:09.90; 15 Matt NEAL (Ford Mondeo Ghia), 23:30.60; 16 Richard KAYE (Ford Mondeo Ghia), 23:38.67; **Retired:** Derek WARWICK (Alfa Romeo 155), 15 laps, handling; David BRABHAM (BMW 318iS), 13 laps, accident; Patrick WATTS (Peugeot 405), 8 laps, accident; Tim SUGDEN (Toyota Carina E), 3 laps, engine; Will HOY (Renault Laguna), 0 laps, vibration.

13/14 May
QUALIFYING

	ROUND 7			ROUND 8	
1	Rickard RYDELL	1:00.954	1	Rickard RYDELL	1:00.786
2	Kelvin BURT	1:01.134	2	Paul RADISICH	1:01.116
3	Paul RADISICH	1:01.184	3	David LESLIE	1:01.290
4	Alain MENU	1:01.253	4	Kelvin BURT	1:01.303
5	John CLELAND	1:01.459	5	Alain MENU	1:01.310
6	Will HOY	1:01.532	6	Tim HARVEY	1:01.425
7	Tim SUGDEN	1:01.553	7	John CLELAND	1:01.426
8	James THOMPSON	1:01.559	8	Tim SUGDEN	1:01.443
9	Patrick WATTS	1:01.565	9	Julian BAILEY	1:01.454
10	David LESLIE	1:01.565	10	Patrick WATTS	1:01.477
11	Tim HARVEY	1:01.613	11	Will HOY	1:01.477
12	Matt NEAL	1:01.639	12	James THOMPSON	1:01.480
13	Julian BAILEY	1:01.726	13	Giampiero SIMONI	1:01.539
14	Giampiero SIMONI	1:01.788	14	Matt NEAL	1:01.566
15	James KAYE	1:01.898	15	Simon HARRISON	1:01.665
16	David BRABHAM	1:01.941	16	James KAYE	1:01.723
17	Simon HARRISON	1:01.977	17	David BRABHAM	1:01.806
18	Johnny CECOTTO	1:02.072	18	Johnny CECOTTO	1:02.000
19	Derek WARWICK	1:02.139	19	Derek WARWICK	1:02.105
20	Nigel SMITH	1:02.339	20	Nigel SMITH	1:02.204
21	Richard KAYE	1:02.468	21	Richard KAYE	1:02.691
22	Hamish IRVINE	1:04.982	22	Hamish IRVINE	1:04.993

RESULTS - ROUND 7
25 laps, 41.05 miles

			Time/laps	Best lap
1	Rickard RYDELL	Volvo 850 20V	25:58.88	1:01.46
2	Paul RADISICH	Ford Mondeo Ghia	26:00.38	1:01.29
3	John CLELAND	Vauxhall Cavalier 16V	26:06.52	1:01.91
4	James THOMPSON	Vauxhall Cavalier 16V	26:07.21	1:01.99
5	Will HOY	Renault Laguna	26:10.60	1:01.88
6	Patrick WATTS	Peugeot 405	26:11.71	1:02.14
7	Tim HARVEY	Volvo 850 20V	26:15.51	1:02.09
8	David BRABHAM	BMW 318iS	26:15.78	1:02.21
9	David LESLIE	Honda Accord	26:18.17	1:02.05
10	James KAYE	Honda Accord	26:20.53	1:02.15

11 Johnny CECOTTO (BMW 318iS), 26:23.95; 12 Simon HARRISON (Peugeot 405), 26:25.03; 13 Matt NEAL (Ford Mondeo Ghia), 26:29.51; 14 Richard KAYE (Ford Mondeo Ghia), 26:47.53; 15 Hamish IRVINE (Peugeot 405), 24 laps; 16 Derek WARWICK (Alfa Romeo 155), 14 laps; **Retired:** Tim SUGDEN (Toyota Carina E), 24 laps, gearbox; Giampiero SIMONI (Alfa Romeo 155), 23 laps, hub; Nigel SMITH (Vauxhall Cavalier 16v), 20 laps, electrics; Julian BAILEY (Toyota Carina E), 20 laps, misfire; Alain MENU (Renault Laguna), 3 laps, driveshaft; Kelvin BURT (Ford Mondeo Ghia), 1 lap, accident.

RESULTS - ROUND 8
22 laps, 36.12 miles

			Time/laps	Best lap
1	Paul RADISICH	Ford Mondeo Ghia	22:51.41	1:01.50
2	Rickard RYDELL	Volvo 850 20V	22:51.84	1:01.62
3	Tim HARVEY	Volvo 850 20V	22:58.70	1:01.92
4	Alain MENU	Renault Laguna	23:00.16	1:01.94
5	John CLELAND	Vauxhall Cavalier 16V	23:02.13	1:01.90
6	Tim SUGDEN	Toyota Carina E	23:02.83	1:01.98
7	Kelvin BURT	Ford Mondeo Ghia	23:03.46	1:01.65
8	David LESLIE	Honda Accord	23:04.02	1:01.94
9	Giampiero SIMONI	Alfa Romeo 155	23:04.45	1:01.96
10	Patrick WATTS	Peugeot 405	23:04.93	1:01.87

11 David BRABHAM (BMW 318iS), 23:07.81; 12 Johnny CECOTTO (BMW 318iS), 23:08.84; 13 James KAYE (Honda Accord), 23:10.72; 14 Matt NEAL (Ford Mondeo Ghia), 23:14.86; 15 Will HOY (Renault Laguna), 23:16.86; 16 Simon HARRISON (Peugeot 405), 21 laps; 17 Derek WARWICK (Alfa Romeo 155), 21 laps; 18 Richard KAYE (Ford Mondeo Ghia), 16 laps; **Retired:** Hamish IRVINE (Peugeot 405), 14 laps, engine; Nigel SMITH (Vauxhall Cavalier 16v), 4 laps, distributor James THOMPSON (Vauxhall Cavalier 16V), 3 laps, accident.

Round 9 & 10 - OULTON PARK

28/29 May
QUALIFYING

	ROUND 9				ROUND 10	
1	James THOMPSON	1:42.186		1	Rickard RYDELL	1:42.626
2	Rickard RYDELL	1:42.373		2	Alain MENU	1:42.721
3	Kelvin BURT	1:42.500		3	James THOMPSON	1:42.733
4	John CLELAND	1:42.503		4	John CLELAND	1:42.990
5	Alain MENU	1:42.533		5	Kelvin BURT	1:43.461
6	Paul RADISICH	1:42.599		6	Julian BAILEY	1:43.519
7	David LESLIE	1:42.819		7	Paul RADISICH	1:43.543
8	Tim SUGDEN	1:43.049		8	Simon HARRISON	1:43.594
9	Julian BAILEY	1:43.052		9	Giampiero SIMONI	1:43.671
10	Simon HARRISON	1:43.284		10	David LESLIE	1:43.728
11	Will HOY	1:43.303		11	Tim SUGDEN	1:43.834
12	Patrick WATTS	1:43.321		12	Johnny CECOTTO	1:43.837
13	Giampiero SIMONI	1:43.402		13	James KAYE	1:43.894
14	Derek WARWICK	1:43.403		14	Derek WARWICK	1:44.023
15	Johnny CECOTTO	1:43.546		15	Patrick WATTS	1:44.247
16	Matt NEAL	1:43.552		16	Will HOY	1:44.346
17	Tim HARVEY	1:43.577		17	Matt NEAL	1:44.486
18	David BRABHAM	1:43.715		18	David BRABHAM	1:44.545
19	Gabriele TARQUINI	1:43.811		19	Tim HARVEY	1:44.679
20	James KAYE	1:43.877		20	Richard KAYE	1:44.767
21	Richard KAYE	1:44.638		21	Gabriele TARQUINI	1:47.239
22	Nigel SMITH	1:46.109		22	Hamish IRVINE	1:50.417
23	Hamish IRVINE	1:52.153				

Rounds 11 & 12 - BRANDS HATCH

10/11 June
QUALIFYING

	ROUND 11				ROUND 12	
1	Alain MENU	1:29.181		1	Alain MENU	1:29.062
2	James THOMPSON	1:29.336		2	James THOMPSON	1:29.199
3	Rickard RYDELL	1:29.401		3	John CLELAND	1:29.220
4	Will HOY	1:29.431		4	Rickard RYDELL	1:29.421
5	John CLELAND	1:29.491		5	Will HOY	1:29.451
6	Paul RADISICH	1:29.501		6	Paul RADISICH	1:29.577
7	Kelvin BURT	1:29.550		7	Tim HARVEY	1:29.581
8	Tim HARVEY	1:29.567		8	Julian BAILEY	1:29.788
9	Patrick WATTS	1:30.056		9	Patrick WATTS	1:29.879
10	Tim SUGDEN	1:30.086		10	Johnny CECOTTO	1:29.905
11	David BRABHAM	1:30.124		11	Tim SUGDEN	1:30.017
12	David LESLIE	1:30.235		12	David LESLIE	1:30.069
13	Julian BAILEY	1:30.359		13	David BRABHAM	1:30.121
14	James KAYE	1:30.368		14	Derek WARWICK	1:30.314
15	Simon HARRISON	1:30.460		15	Matt NEAL	1:30.395
16	Johnny CECOTTO	1:30.485		16	Simon HARRISON	1:30.495
17	Giampiero SIMONI	1:30.585		17	Giampiero SIMONI	1:30.622
18	Derek WARWICK	1:30.847		18	Nigel SMITH	1:31.277
19	Matt NEAL	1:30.849		19	Richard KAYE	1:32.519
20	Nigel SMITH	1:30.976		20	Hamish IRVINE	1:34.197
21	Richard KAYE	1:33.760		21	James KAYE	1:50.297
22	Hamish IRVINE	1:34.395				

RESULTS - ROUND 9
13 laps, 36.01 miles

			Time/laps	Best lap
1	Rickard RYDELL	Volvo 850 20v	22:39.09	1:43.85
2	John CLELAND	Vauxhall Cavalier 16V	22:39.61	1:43.63
3	Alain MENU	Renault Laguna	22:41.20	1:43.61
4	Julian BAILEY	Toyota Carina E	22:49.00	1:44.28
5	Giampiero SIMONI	Alfa Romeo 155	22:51.84	1:44.25
6	James THOMPSON	Vauxhall Cavalier 16V	22:52.34	1:44.39
7	Simon HARRISON	Peugeot 405	22:53.43	1:44.40
8	Tim HARVEY	Volvo 850 20v	22:56.09	1:44.46
9	Johnny CECOTTO	BMW 318	22:56.60	1:44.54
10	David BRABHAM	BMW 318	23:00.33	1:44.56

11 Gabriele TARQUINI (Alfa Romeo 155), 23:06.58; 12 Nigel SMITH (Vauxhall Cavalier), 23:13.14; 13 Matt NEAL (Ford Mondeo), 23:13.59; 14 James KAYE (Honda Accord), 23:14.86; 15 Richard KAYE (Ford Mondeo), 23:24.73; 16 Hamish IRVINE (Peugeot 405), 23:50.72; **Retired:** Will HOY (Renault Laguna), 7 laps, oil pump; Paul RADISICH (Ford Mondeo Ghia), 1 lap, accident; Tim SUGDEN (Toyota Carina E), 1 lap, accident; Patrick WATTS (Peugeot 405), 0 lap, accident.

RESULTS - ROUND 11
8 + 5 laps, 33.80 miles

			Time/laps	Best lap
1	Alain MENU	Renault Laguna	22:34.60	1:42.22
2	John CLELAND	Vauxhall Cavalier 16V	22:35.95	1:42.12
3	Tim HARVEY	Volvo 850 20v	22:40.06	1:42.70
4	Will HOY	Renault Laguna	22:48.32	1:42.38
5	Patrick WATTS	Peugeot 405	22:59.82	1:43.77
6	Julian BAILEY	Toyota Carina E	23:01.73	1:43.19
7	Rickard RYDELL	Volvo 850 20v	23:03.13	1:43.22
8	Derek WARWICK	Alfa Romeo 155	23:03.97	1:42.88
9	Giampiero SIMONI	Alfa Romeo 155	23:07.73	1:43.48
10	Johnny CECOTTO	BMW 318	23:18.96	1:43.44

11 Simon HARRISON (Peugeot 405), 23:35.10; 12 David LESLIE (Honda Accord), 23:35.23; 13 James KAYE (Honda Accord), 23:41.9.; 14 Hamish IRVINE (Peugeot 405), 24:04.13; 15 Richard KAYE (Ford Mondeo), 24:15.01; 16 Nigel SMITH (Vauxhall Cavalier), 11 laps; **Retired:** Tim SUGDEN (Toyota Carina E), 8 laps, accident; James THOMPSON (Vauxhall Cavalier 16V), 2 laps, accident; Kelvin BURT (Ford Mondeo Ghia), 1 lap, accident; Paul RADISICH (Ford Mondeo Ghia), 0 laps, accident; David BRABHAM (BMW 318), 0 laps, accident; Matt NEAL (Ford Mondeo), 0 laps, accident.

RESULTS - ROUND 10
16 laps, 44.32 miles

			Time/laps	Best lap
1	Alain MENU	Renault Laguna	27:47.01	1:43.07
2	Rickard RYDELL	Volvo 850 20v	27:48.84	1:43.40
3	John CLELAND	Vauxhall Cavalier 16V	27:49.65	1:43.37
4	James THOMPSON	Vauxhall Cavalier 16V	28:02.10	1:43.77
5	Paul RADISICH	Ford Mondeo Ghia	28:05.08	1:43.99
6	Kelvin BURT	Ford Mondeo Ghia	28:07.63	1:43.97
7	Tim HARVEY	Volvo 850 20v	28:11.99	1:44.39
8	Giampiero SIMONI	Alfa Romeo 155	28:12.52	1:44.34
9	David BRABHAM	BMW 318	28:12.71	1:43.94
10	Julian BAILEY	Toyota Carina E	28:20.47	1:43.87

11 James KAYE (Honda Accord), 28:20.48; 12 Tim SUGDEN (Toyota Carina E), 28:20.49; 13 Simon HARRISON (Peugeot 405), 28:21.95; 14 Patrick WATTS (Peugeot 405), 28:27.93; 15 Matt NEAL (Ford Mondeo), 28:31.14; 16 Nigel SMITH (Vauxhall Cavalier), 28:45.15; 17 Richard KAYE (Ford Mondeo), 29:07.51; 18 Will HOY (Renault Laguna), 28:14.85; **Retired:** Hamish IRVINE (Peugeot 405), 9 laps, engine; Johnny CECOTTO (BMW 318), 1 laps. suspension; Gabriele TARQUINI (Alfa Romeo 155), 0 laps, accident.

RESULTS - ROUND 12
10 laps, 26.00 miles

			Time/laps	Best lap
1	John CLELAND	Vauxhall Cavalier 16V	17:39.02	1:44.97
2	James THOMPSON	Vauxhall Cavalier 16V	17:39.64	1:44.62
3	Alain MENU	Renault Laguna	17:39.99	1:44.45
4	Will HOY	Renault Laguna	17:40.72	1:44.49
5	Tim HARVEY	Volvo 850 20v	17:41.24	1:44.68
6	Julian BAILEY	Toyota Carina E	17:43.62	1:44.67
7	Paul RADISICH	Ford Mondeo Ghia	17:44.37	1:44.60
8	Patrick WATTS	Peugeot 405	17:49.07	1:45.15
9	Johnny CECOTTO	BMW 318	17:52.38	1:45.62
10	David BRABHAM	BMW 318	17:55.55	1:46.16

11 Derek WARWICK (Alfa Romeo 155), 17:56.06; 12 Giampiero SIMONI (Alfa Romeo 155), 17:57.14; 13 Simon HARRISON (Peugeot 405), 17:59.12; 14 Kelvin BURT (Ford Mondeo Ghia), 17:59.69; 15 Richard KAYE (Ford Mondeo), 18:21.48; 16 Hamish IRVINE (Peugeot 405), 18:21.50; 17 Nigel SMITH (Vauxhall Cavalier), 18:42.44; 18 David LESLIE (Honda Accord), 18:45.27; 19 James KAYE (Honda Accord), 18:46.18.

118

24/25 June
QUALIFYING

ROUND 13			ROUND 14		
1	John CLELAND	1:37.730	1	John CLELAND	1:38.044
2	James THOMPSON	1:37.786	2	Kelvin BURT	1:38.139
3	David LESLIE	1:37.893	3	Paul RADISICH	1:38.203
4	Rickard RYDELL	1:37.934	4	Rickard RYDELL	1:38.256
5	Alain MENU	1:38.215	5	James THOMPSON	1:38.318
6	Paul RADISICH	1:38.402	6	Alain MENU	1:38.392
7	Julian BAILEY	1:38.461	7	David LESLIE	1:38.412
8	Derek WARWICK	1:38.465	8	Julian BAILEY	1:38.627
9	James KAYE	1:38.572	9	Johnny CECOTTO	1:38.666
10	Tim HARVEY	1:38.585	10	James KAYE	1:38.799
11	Kelvin BURT	1:38.616	11	Tim SUGDEN	1:38.963
12	Tim SUGDEN	1:38.745	12	Tim HARVEY	1:39.058
13	David BRABHAM	1:38.879	13	Patrick WATTS	1:39.239
14	Patrick WATTS	1:38.889	14	Derek WARWICK	1:39.246
15	Matt NEAL	1:38.898	15	Matt NEAL	1:39.282
16	Giampiero SIMONI	1:38.926	16	Giampiero SIMONI	1:39.289
17	Johnny CECOTTO	1:38.951	17	Will HOY	1:39.450
18	Simon HARRISON	1:39.021	18	Simon HARRISON	1:39.451
19	Will HOY	1:39.261	19	David BRABHAM	1:39.611
20	Nigel SMITH	1:41.255	20	Nigel SMITH	1:40.534
21	Richard KAYE	1:41.875	21	Richard KAYE	1:41.753
22	Hamish IRVINE	1:42.199	22	Hamish IRVINE	1:42.586

15/16 July
QUALIFYING

ROUND 15		
1	John CLELAND	1:59.647
2	Alain MENU	1:59.805
3	Paul RADISICH	1:59.910
4	James THOMPSON	1:59.927
5	Rickard RYDELL	2:00.045
6	Will HOY	2:00.178
7	David LESLIE	2:00.273
8	Tim HARVEY	2:00.403
9	Kelvin BURT	2:00.469
10	Julian BAILEY	2:00.514
11	Giampiero SIMONI	2:00.655
12	Johnny CECOTTO	2:00.802
13	James KAYE	2:00.906
14	David BRABHAM	2:01.059
15	Patrick WATTS	2:01.168
16	Derek WARWICK	2:01.206
17	Matt NEAL	2:01.362
18	Tim SUGDEN	2:01.363
19	Simon HARRISON	2:01.439
20	Nigel SMITH	2:02.535
21	Robb GRAVETT	2:02.986
22	Richard KAYE	2:03.170
23	Hamish IRVINE	2:06.052

RESULTS - ROUND 13
15 laps, 37.50 miles

			Time/laps	Best lap
1	John CLELAND	Vauxhall Cavalier 16V	25:01.93	1:39.02
2	Rickard RYDELL	Volvo 850 20v	25:04.60	1:39.59
3	Alain MENU	Renault Laguna	25:08.93	1:39.62
4	James THOMPSON	Vauxhall Cavalier 16V	25:09.46	1:39.27
5	Paul RADISICH	Ford Mondeo Ghia	25:13.87	1:39.56
6	Julian BAILEY	Toyota Carina E	25:14.36	1:39.38
7	David LESLIE	Honda Accord	25:19.89	1:39.84
8	Tim SUGDEN	Toyota Carina E	25:20.51	1:40.27
9	Kelvin BURT	Ford Mondeo Ghia	25:21.32	1:39.50
10	Tim HARVEY	Volvo 850 20v	25:24.60	1:40.19

11 David BRABHAM (BMW 318), 25:24.87; 12 Will HOY (Renault Laguna), 25:26.23; 13 Derek WARWICK (Alfa Romeo 155), 25:29.81; 14 James KAYE (Honda Accord), 25:31.12; 15 Patrick WATTS (Peugeot 405), 25:37.96; 16 Nigel SMITH (Vauxhall Cavalier), 25:59.64; 17 Richard KAYE (Ford Mondeo), 26:06.60; 18 Hamish IRVINE (Peugeot 405), 26:16.53; **Retired:** Simon HARRISON (Peugeot 405), 9 laps, handling; Johnny CECOTTO (BMW 318), 2 laps, accident; Matt NEAL (Ford Mondeo), 2 laps, accident; Giampiero SIMONI (Alfa Romeo 155), 2 laps, steering.

RESULTS - ROUND 15
15 laps, 47.13 miles

			Time/laps	Best lap
1	John CLELAND	Vauxhall Cavalier 16V	33:47.70	2:13.68
2	Will HOY	Renault Laguna	33:55.27	2:13.98
3	James THOMPSON	Vauxhall Cavalier 16V	33:56.96	2:13.53
4	Julian BAILEY	Toyota Carina E	33:57.48	2:13.39
5	Kelvin BURT	Ford Mondeo Ghia	34:01.64	2:13.76
6	Paul RADISICH	Ford Mondeo Ghia	34:15.51	2:15.20
7	David BRABHAM	BMW 318	34:23.28	2:16.19
8	Tim SUGDEN	Toyota Carina E	34:24.99	2:15.22
9	Derek WARWICK	Alfa Romeo 155	34:31.63	2:16.60
10	Patrick WATTS	Peugeot 405	34:33.72	2:16.16

11 Giampiero SIMONI (Alfa Romeo 155), 34:34.01; 12 David LESLIE (Honda Accord), 34:41.74; 13 Robb GRAVETT (Ford Mondeo Ghia), 34:46.10; 14 Matt NEAL (Ford Mondeo), 34:48.72; 15 Simon HARRISON (Peugeot 405), 34:50.83; 16 Alain MENU (Renault Laguna), 34:52.21; 17 Rickard RYDELL (Volvo 850 20v), 35:24.44; 18 Hamish IRVINE (Peugeot 405), 35:59.77; **Retired:** Tim HARVEY (Volvo 850 20v), 11 laps, accident; James KAYE (Honda Accord), 8 laps, accident; Nigel SMITH (Vauxhall Cavalier), 7 laps, alternator; Richard KAYE (Ford Mondeo), 0 laps, clutch.

RESULTS - ROUND 14
15 laps, 37.50 miles

			Time/laps	Best lap
1	John CLELAND	Vauxhall Cavalier 16V	25:05.02	1:39.16
2	Paul RADISICH	Ford Mondeo Ghia	25:11.03	1:39.41
3	Kelvin BURT	Ford Mondeo Ghia	25:12.88	1:39.80
4	Alain MENU	Renault Laguna	25:14.27	1:39.81
5	James THOMPSON	Vauxhall Cavalier 16V	25:16.21	1:39.77
6	Rickard RYDELL	Volvo 850 20v	25:16.85	1:39.85
7	Julian BAILEY	Toyota Carina E	25:17.03	1:39.70
8	Will HOY	Renault Laguna	25:21.18	1:39.74
9	David LESLIE	Honda Accord	25:23.55	1:39.93
10	James KAYE	Honda Accord	25:23.93	1:40.14

11 David BRABHAM (BMW 318), 25:24.32; 12 Tim HARVEY (Volvo 850 20v), 25:28.51; 13 Tim SUGDEN (Toyota Carina E), 26:04.60; 14 Richard KAYE (Ford Mondeo), 26:04.72; 15 Hamish IRVINE (Peugeot 405), 26:06.07; **Retired:** Derek WARWICK (Alfa Romeo 155), 8 laps, accident; Giampiero SIMONI (Alfa Romeo 155), 6 laps, accident; Patrick WATTS (Peugeot 405), 5 laps, accident; Simon HARRISON (Peugeot 405), 4 laps, fire; Nigel SMITH (Vauxhall Cavalier), 4 laps, accident; Matt NEAL (Ford Mondeo), 3 laps, accident; Johnny CECOTTO (BMW 318), 2 laps accident.

UNISYS

Rounds 16 & 17 - KNOCKHILL

29/30 July
QUALIFYING

	ROUND 16			ROUND 17	
1	Rickard RYDELL	0:53.463	1	Rickard RYDELL	0:53.751
2	Alain MENU	0:53.949	2	Alain MENU	0:53.902
3	Paul RADISICH	0:53.958	3	Tim HARVEY	0:54.049
4	Tim HARVEY	0:53.993	4	Paul RADISICH	0:54.208
5	Kelvin BURT	0:54.153	5	Kelvin BURT	0:54.303
6	Julian BAILEY	0:54.157	6	James KAYE	0:54.356
7	John CLELAND	0:54.158	7	Julian BAILEY	0:54.371
8	David LESLIE	0:54.198	8	John CLELAND	0:54.418
9	James KAYE	0:54.227	9	David LESLIE	0:54.462
10	David BRABHAM	0:54.298	10	David BRABHAM	0:54.469
11	Will HOY	0:54.395	11	Will HOY	0:54.557
12	Johnny CECOTTO	0:54.399	12	Johnny CECOTTO	0:54.569
13	Simon HARRISON	0:54.479	13	Tim SUGDEN	0:54.589
14	Gabriele TARQUINI	0:54.509	14	Gabriele TARQUINI	0:54.758
15	Robb GRAVETT	0:54.511	15	Derek WARWICK	0:54.794
16	Matt NEAL	0:54.522	16	Patrick WATTS	0:54.805
17	Tim SUGDEN	0:54.573	17	Matt NEAL	0:54.834
18	Jeff ALLAM	0:54.679	18	Richard KAYE	0:54.851
19	Derek WARWICK	0:54.693	19	Robb GRAVETT	0:55.000
20	Richard KAYE	0:54.957	20	Jeff ALLAM	0:55.029
21	Nigel SMITH	0:55.460	21	Simon HARRISON	0:55.250
22	Hamish IRVINE	0:55.937	22	Nigel SMITH	0:55.933
23	Patrick WATTS	0:58.743	23	Hamish IRVINE	0:56.488

RESULTS - ROUND 16
31 laps, 40.30 miles

			Time/laps	Best lap
1	Rickard RYDELL	Volvo 850 20V	28:53.85	0:54.59
2	Tim HARVEY	Volvo 850 20V	29:00.82	0:54.88
3	Kelvin BURT	Ford Mondeo Ghia	29:01.79	0:55.17
4	Johnny CECOTTO	BMW 318iS	29:02.29	0:55.25
5	John CLELAND	Vauxhall Cavalier 16V	29:03.51	0:55.12
6	Julian BAILEY	Toyota Carina E	29:04.36	0:55.27
7	Tim SUGDEN	Toyota Carina E	29:06.35	0:55.41
8	Jeff ALLAM	Vauxhall Cavalier 16V	29:07.32	0:55.29
9	Matt NEAL	Ford Mondeo Ghia	29:12.55	0:55.48
10	Robb GRAVETT	Ford Mondeo Ghia	29:28.08	0:55.67

11 David LESLIE (Honda Accord), 29:38.17; 12 Nigel SMITH (Vauxhall Cavalier 16v), 28:57.05; 13 Richard KAYE (Ford Mondeo Ghia), 29:23.78; 14 Hamish IRVINE (Peugeot 405), 29:45.62; **Retired:** Paul RADISICH (Ford Mondeo Ghia), 29 laps, accident; Will HOY (Renault Laguna), 29 laps, accident; Gabriele TARQUINI (Alfa Romeo 155), 25 laps, hub; Alain MENU (Renault Laguna), 13 laps, gearbox; James KAYE (Honda Accord), 6 laps, accident; Simon HARRISON (Peugeot 405), 2 laps, accident; Derek WARWICK (Alfa Romeo 155), 2 laps, accident

RESULTS - ROUND 17
32 laps, 41.60 miles

			Time/laps	Best lap
1	Alain MENU	Renault Laguna	29:27.65	0:54.67
2	Rickard RYDELL	Volvo 850 20V	29:30.51	0:54.73
3	Tim HARVEY	Volvo 850 20V	29:46.84	0:54.65
4	David BRABHAM	BMW 318iS	29:52.20	0:55.10
5	James KAYE	Honda Accord	29:53.55	0:54.86
6	John CLELAND	Vauxhall Cavalier 16V	29:53.62	0:54.99
7	David LESLIE	Honda Accord	29:55.77	0:55.18
8	Gabriele TARQUINI	Alfa Romeo 155	29:58.45	0:55.23
9	Julian BAILEY	Toyota Carina E	30:00.02	0:55.49
10	Tim SUGDEN	Toyota Carina E	30:06.09	0:55.61

11 Patrick WATTS (Peugeot 405), 30:10.14; 12 Jeff ALLAM (Vauxhall Cavalier 16V), 30:12.56; 13 Matt NEAL (Ford Mondeo Ghia), 30:13.64; 14 Robb GRAVETT (Ford Mondeo Ghia), 30:20.14; 15 Richard KAYE (Ford Mondeo Ghia), 30:21.52; 16 Derek WARWICK (Alfa Romeo 155), 30:23.39; 17 Hamish IRVINE (Peugeot 405), 29:50.76; 18 Nigel SMITH (Vauxhall Cavalier 16v), 29:40.32; **Retired:** Paul RADISICH (Ford Mondeo Ghia), 30 laps, tyre; Will HOY (Renault Laguna), 18 laps, gearbox; Simon HARRISON (Peugeot 405), 9 laps, accident; Johnny CECOTTO (BMW 318iS), 6 laps, accident; Kelvin BURT (Ford Mondeo Ghia), 4 laps, accident.

Round 18 & 19 - BRANDS HATCH

12/13 August
QUALIFYING

	ROUND 18			ROUND 19	
1	Rickard RYDELL	0:46.643	1	Rickard RYDELL	0:46.646
2	John CLELAND	0:46.723	2	John CLELAND	0:46.680
3	Will HOY	0:46.793	3	Will HOY	0:46.722
4	Paul RADISICH	0:46.836	4	Paul RADISICH	0:46.802
5	Johnny CECOTTO	0:46.844	5	Johnny CECOTTO	0:46.895
6	Tim HARVEY	0:46.868	6	David BRABHAM	0:46.973
7	Alain MENU	0:46.915	7	Patrick WATTS	0:46.979
8	Derek WARWICK	0:46.918	8	Alain MENU	0:46.997
9	Mike BRIGGS	0:46.920	9	Gabriele TARQUINI	0:47.018
10	James KAYE	0:47.009	10	Mike BRIGGS	0:47.067
11	David LESLIE	0:47.042	11	Tim HARVEY	0:47.076
12	Julian BAILEY	0:47.051	12	James KAYE	0:47.077
13	Patrick WATTS	0:47.122	13	Julian BAILEY	0:47.094
14	Kelvin BURT	0:47.191	14	David LESLIE	0:47.106
15	Simon HARRISON	0:47.192	15	Kelvin BURT	0:47.150
16	David BRABHAM	0:47.267	16	Matt NEAL	0:47.242
17	Matt NEAL	0:47.304	17	Simon HARRISON	0:47.293
18	Tim SUGDEN	0:47.391	18	Tim SUGDEN	0:47.312
19	Robb GRAVETT	0:47.523	19	Robb GRAVETT	0:47.469
20	Nigel SMITH	0:47.587	20	Derek WARWICK	0:47.484
21	Richard KAYE	0:47.858	21	Richard KAYE	0:47.597
22	Charlie COX	0:48.183	22	Nigel SMITH	0:47.832
23	Hamish IRVINE	0:49.221	23	Charlie COX	0:48.258
24	Gabriele TARQUINI	1:12.410	24	Hamish IRVINE	0:49.348

RESULTS - ROUND 18
30 laps, 36.92 miles

			Time/laps	Best lap
1	Will HOY	Renault Laguna	23:51.57	0:47.04
2	Rickard RYDELL	Volvo 850 20V	23:52.03	0:46.90
3	John CLELAND	Vauxhall Cavalier 16V	23:52.27	0:46.94
4	Alain MENU	Renault Laguna	23:52.75	0:46.94
5	Johnny CECOTTO	BMW 318iS	23:53.18	0:46.91
6	Mike BRIGGS	Vauxhall Cavalier 16V	24:01.27	0:47.28
7	Tim HARVEY	Volvo 850 20V	24:04.82	0:47.52
8	Derek WARWICK	Alfa Romeo 155	24:09.08	0:47.44
9	Julian BAILEY	Toyota Carina E	24:09.28	0:47.06
10	James KAYE	Honda Accord	24:12.11	0:47.19

11 Patrick WATTS (Peugeot 405), 24:14.68; 12 Tim SUGDEN (Toyota Carina E), 24:14.94; 13 Kelvin BURT (Ford Mondeo Ghia), 24:21.67; 14 Paul RADISICH (Ford Mondeo Ghia), 24:22.78; 15 Matt NEAL (Ford Mondeo Ghia), 24:23.06; 16 Nigel SMITH (Vauxhall Cavalier 16v), 24:23.50; 17 David LESLIE (Honda Accord), 24:28.06; 18 Richard KAYE (Ford Mondeo Ghia), 24:36.11; 19 Robb GRAVETT (Ford Mondeo Ghia), 24:37.39; 20 Hamish IRVINE (Peugeot 405), 28 laps; 21 Charlie COX (Ford Mondeo Ghia), 28 laps; **Retired:** Gabriele TARQUINI (Alfa Romeo 155), 27 laps, cooling; David BRABHAM (BMW 318iS), 26 laps, tyre; Simon HARRISON (Peugeot 405), 12 laps, engine.

RESULTS - ROUND 19
30 laps, 36.92 miles

			Time/laps	Best lap
1	John CLELAND	Vauxhall Cavalier 16V	23:46.09	0:46.82
2	Will HOY	Renault Laguna	23:53.93	0:47.09
3	Rickard RYDELL	Volvo 850 20V	23:55.72	0:47.06
4	Gabriele TARQUINI	Alfa Romeo 155	23:56.11	0:47.23
5	Mike BRIGGS	Vauxhall Cavalier 16V	23:56.45	0:47.09
6	Patrick WATTS	Peugeot 405	24:05.05	0:47.58
7	Tim HARVEY	Volvo 850 20V	24:06.73	0:47.29
8	James KAYE	Honda Accord	24:10.72	0:47.35
9	Tim SUGDEN	Toyota Carina E	24:10.98	0:47.42
10	David LESLIE	Honda Accord	24:18.04	0:47.31

11 Kelvin BURT (Ford Mondeo Ghia), 24:20.08; 12 Matt NEAL (Ford Mondeo Ghia), 24:20.39; 13 Robb GRAVETT (Ford Mondeo Ghia), 24:20.77; 14 Derek WARWICK (Alfa Romeo 155), 24:22.44; 15 Charlie COX (Ford Mondeo Ghia), 24:30.84; 16 Nigel SMITH (Vauxhall Cavalier 16v), 24:31.10; 17 Richard KAYE (Ford Mondeo Ghia), 29 laps; 18 Alain MENU (Renault Laguna), 18 laps; **Retired:** Paul RADISICH (Ford Mondeo Ghia), 19 laps, accident; Julian BAILEY (Toyota Carina E), 13 laps, accident; David BRABHAM (BMW 318iS), 5 laps, oil line; Johnny CECOTTO (BMW 318iS), 1 lap, accident; Hamish IRVINE (Peugeot 405), 0 laps, accident.

20 & 21 August
QUALIFYING

	ROUND 20				ROUND 21	
1	Rickard RYDELL	1:12.369		1	Rickard RYDELL	1:12.137
2	Alain MENU	1:12.386		2	Alain MENU	1:12.603
3	John CLELAND	1:12.507		3	Tim HARVEY	1:12.686
4	Tim HARVEY	1:12.559		4	Will HOY	1:12.695
5	Julian BAILEY	1:12.799		5	Matt NEAL	1:12.736
6	James KAYE	1:12.800		6	John CLELAND	1:12.821
7	Paul RADISICH	1:12.827		7	Tim SUGDEN	1:12.857
8	Robb GRAVETT	1:12.835		8	Mike BRIGGS	1:12.916
9	Kelvin BURT	1:12.920		9	Paul RADISICH	1:12.931
10	Johnny CECOTTO	1:12.938		10	Simon HARRISON	1:12.970
11	Matt NEAL	1:12.959		11	James KAYE	1:13.030
12	Will HOY	1:13.016		12	Julian BAILEY	1:13.035
13	Simon HARRISON	1:13.032		13	David BRABHAM	1:13.113
14	Tim SUGDEN	1:13.051		14	David LESLIE	1:13.154
15	David LESLIE	1:13.083		15	Johnny CECOTTO	1:13.180
16	David BRABHAM	1:13.187		16	Kelvin BURT	1:13.265
17	Mike BRIGGS	1:13.209		17	Robb GRAVETT	1:13.437
18	Patrick WATTS	1:13.227		18	Gabriele TARQUINI	1:13.676
19	Richard KAYE	1:13.457		19	Richard KAYE	1:13.779
20	Gabriele TARQUINI	1:13.844		20	Charlie COX	1:14.135
21	Charlie COX	1:13.947		21	Patrick WATTS	1:14.298
22	Derek WARWICK	1:14.303		22	Derek WARWICK	1:14.342
23	Nigel SMITH	1:14.859		23	Nigel SMITH	1:14.473
24	Hamish IRVINE	1:15.566		24	Hamish IRVINE	1:15.049

9 & 10 September
QUALIFYING

	ROUND 22				ROUND 23	
1	Alain MENU	1:00.915		1	Alain MENU	1:00.344
2	John CLELAND	1:00.919		2	John CLELAND	1:00.455
3	Julian BAILEY	1:01.170		3	David LESLIE	1:00.506
4	Will HOY	1:01.206		4	Tim HARVEY	1:00.669
5	David LESLIE	1:01.249		5	Julian BAILEY	1:00.680
6	Rickard RYDELL	1:01.288		6	Will HOY	1:00.754
7	James KAYE	1:01.520		7	James KAYE	1:00.773
8	Gabriele TARQUINI	1:01.535		8	Johnny CECOTTO	1:00.805
9	Tim HARVEY	1:01.603		9	Kelvin BURT	1:00.925
10	Johnny CECOTTO	1:01.645		10	Patrick WATTS	1:00.958
11	Simon HARRISON	1:01.688		11	Gabriele TARQUINI	1:00.992
12	Paul RADISICH	1:01.699		12	Mike BRIGGS	1:01.039
13	Mike BRIGGS	1:01.721		13	Simon HARRISON	1:01.081
14	Patrick WATTS	1:01.730		14	Matt NEAL	1:01.209
15	Derek WARWICK	1:01.784		15	Derek WARWICK	1:01.235
16	Kelvin BURT	1:01.945		16	Tim SUGDEN	1:01.263
17	Tim SUGDEN	1:02.075		17	David BRABHAM	1:01.315
18	Matt NEAL	1:02.081		18	Rickard RYDELL	1:01.399
19	David BRABHAM	1:02.159		19	Paul RADISICH	1:01.443
20	Rickard RYDELL	1:02.308		20	Nigel SMITH	1:01.536
21	Charlie COX	1:02.556		21	Robb GRAVETT	1:02.137
22	Robb GRAVETT	1:02.606		22	Charlie COX	1:02.488
23	Nigel SMITH	1:02.678		23	Hamish IRVINE	1:02.951
24	Hamish IRVINE	1:04.463				

RESULTS - ROUND 20
18 laps, 35.14 miles

			Time/laps	Best lap
1	Kelvin BURT	Ford Mondeo Ghia	23:57.61	1:15.98
2	Patrick WATTS	Peugeot 405	24:18.29	1:16.16
3	Robb GRAVETT	Ford Mondeo Ghia	24:19.87	1:15.77
4	Gabriele TARQUINI	Alfa Romeo 155	24:22.50	1:16.92
5	Richard KAYE	Ford Mondeo Ghia	24:22.63	1:15.23
6	Tim SUGDEN	Toyota Carina E	24:23.78	1:16.73
7	Mike BRIGGS	Vauxhall Cavalier 16V	24:25.89	1:17.14
8	David LESLIE	Honda Accord	24:27.78	1:16.00
9	Paul RADISICH	Ford Mondeo Ghia	24:35.20	1:20.34
10	Johnny CECOTTO	BMW 318iS	24:46.61	1:14.95

11 Julian BAILEY (Toyota Carina E), 24:46.88; 12 Will HOY (Renault Laguna), 24:48.09; 13 John CLELAND (Vauxhall Cavalier 16V), 24:53.84; 14 Rickard RYDELL (Volvo 850 20V), 24:54.04; 15 Matt NEAL (Ford Mondeo Ghia), 25:00.10 1; 16 David BRABHAM (BMW 318iS), 24:04.71; 17 Nigel SMITH (Vauxhall Cavalier 16v), 24:06.56; 18 James KAYE (Honda Accord), 24:12.15; 19 Simon HARRISON (Peugeot 405), 25:05.27; **Retired:** Charlie COX (Ford Mondeo Ghia), 13 laps, radiator; Hamish IRVINE (Peugeot 405), 11 laps, accident; Alain MENU (Renault Laguna), 2 laps, accident; Tim HARVEY (Volvo 850 20V), 2 laps, accident; Derek WARWICK (Alfa Romeo 155), 1 lap, engine.

RESULTS - ROUND 21
20 laps, 39.04 miles

			Time/laps	Best lap
1	Will HOY	Renault Laguna	24:42.79	1:13.16
2	Tim HARVEY	Volvo 850 20V	24:43.29	1:13.21
3	John CLELAND	Vauxhall Cavalier 16V	24:44.36	1:13.20
4	Matt NEAL	Ford Mondeo Ghia	24:53.82	1:13.77
5	Mike BRIGGS	Vauxhall Cavalier 16V	25:05.79	1:14.02
6	Julian BAILEY	Toyota Carina E	25:05.99	1:13.97
7	Tim SUGDEN	Toyota Carina E	25:06.60	1:13.93
8	David LESLIE	Honda Accord	25:09.86	1:13.90
9	James KAYE	Honda Accord	25:10.24	1:13.75
10	Alain MENU	Renault Laguna	25:11.36	1:13.74

11 Simon HARRISON (Peugeot 405), 25:13.98; 12 Kelvin BURT (Ford Mondeo Ghia), 25:15.83; 13 Derek WARWICK (Alfa Romeo 155), 25:16.86; 14 Richard KAYE (Ford Mondeo Ghia), 25:17.94; 15 Nigel SMITH (Vauxhall Cavalier 16v), 25:31.11; 16 Charlie COX (Ford Mondeo Ghia), 25:43.28; 17 David BRABHAM (BMW 318iS), 19 laps; **Retired:** Johnny CECOTTO (BMW 318iS), 18 laps, accident; Rickard RYDELL (Volvo 850 20V), 14 laps, accident; Paul RADISICH (Ford Mondeo Ghia), 14 laps, tyres; Gabriele TARQUINI (Alfa Romeo 155), 2 laps, tracking; Patrick WATTS (Peugeot 405), 0 laps, fuel systems; Robb GRAVETT (Ford Mondeo Ghia), 0 laps, accident.

RESULTS - ROUND 22
22 laps, 36.30 miles

			Time/laps	Best lap
1	Alain MENU	Renault Laguna	22:48.71	1:01.44
2	Will HOY	Renault Laguna	22:54.21	1:01.80
3	John CLELAND	Vauxhall Cavalier 16V	22:54.92	1:01.73
4	Gabriele TARQUINI	Alfa Romeo 155	22:59.81	1:01.71
5	Rickard RYDELL	Volvo 850 20V	23:00.37	1:01.98
6	David LESLIE	Honda Accord	23:02.06	1:01.92
7	James KAYE	Honda Accord	23:06.79	1:02.17
8	Derek WARWICK	Alfa Romeo 155	23:13.35	1:02.12
9	Simon HARRISON	Peugeot 405	23:14.37	1:02.08
10	Kelvin BURT	Ford Mondeo Ghia	23:16.92	1:02.32

11 David BRABHAM (BMW 318iS), 23:17.19; 12 Mike BRIGGS (Vauxhall Cavalier 16V), 23:17.51; 13 Matt NEAL (Ford Mondeo Ghia), 23:22.03; 14 Nigel SMITH (Vauxhall Cavalier 16v), 23:26.81; 15 Richard KAYE (Ford Mondeo Ghia), 23:27.60; 16 Robb GRAVETT (Ford Mondeo Ghia), 23:35.32; 17 Hamish IRVINE (Peugeot 405), 23:40.32; **Retired:** Tim HARVEY (Volvo 850 20V), 15 laps, engine; Patrick WATTS (Peugeot 405), 13 laps, engine; Julian BAILEY (Toyota Carina E), 13 laps, steering; Johnny CECOTTO (BMW 318iS), 12 laps, damage; Charlie COX (Ford Mondeo Ghia), 6 laps, accident; Paul RADISICH (Ford Mondeo Ghia), 3 laps, fire; Tim SUGDEN (Toyota Carina E), 0 laps, accident.

RESULTS - ROUND 23
24 laps, 39.60 miles

			Time/laps	Best lap
1	Alain MENU	Renault Laguna	26:38.58	1:01.30
2	John CLELAND	Vauxhall Cavalier 16V	26:44.25	1:01.37
3	David LESLIE	Honda Accord	26:44.45	1:01.57
4	Julian BAILEY	Toyota Carina E	26:45.29	1:01.77
5	Tim HARVEY	Volvo 850 20V	26:51.23	1:01.79
6	Johnny CECOTTO	BMW 318iS	26:52.54	1:01.93
7	Kelvin BURT	Ford Mondeo Ghia	26:53.54	1:01.88
8	Mike BRIGGS	Vauxhall Cavalier 16V	26:55.65	1:01.88
9	James KAYE	Honda Accord	26:57.59	1:02.04
10	Rickard RYDELL	Volvo 850 20V	26:57.94	1:01.99

11 Matt NEAL (Ford Mondeo Ghia), 26:59.82; 12 Paul RADISICH (Ford Mondeo Ghia), 27:01.16; 13 Gabriele TARQUINI (Alfa Romeo 155), 27:34.42; 14 Nigel SMITH (Vauxhall Cavalier 16v), 27:38.62 1; 15 Richard KAYE (Ford Mondeo Ghia), 27:43.56 1; 16 Hamish IRVINE (Peugeot 405), 23 laps; **Retired:** David BRABHAM (BMW 318iS), 23 laps, suspension; Simon HARRISON (Peugeot 405), 21 laps, engine; Derek WARWICK (Alfa Romeo 155), 11 laps, accident; Patrick WATTS (Peugeot 405), 2 laps, accident; Will HOY (Renault Laguna), 1 lap, accident; Tim SUGDEN (Toyota Carina E), 0 laps, accident.

23/24 September
QUALIFYING

	ROUND 24			ROUND 25	
1	John CLELAND	1:00.677	1	Alain MENU	1:00.713
2	Alain MENU	1:00.689	2	Will HOY	1:00.851
3	Paul RADISICH	1:00.718	3	David LESLIE	1:00.919
4	Will HOY	1:00.781	4	Paul RADISICH	1:01.069
5	David LESLIE	1:00.872	5	Kelvin BURT	1:01.092
6	Julian BAILEY	1:00.968	6	John CLELAND	1:01.126
7	Kelvin BURT	1:01.051	7	Julian BAILEY	1:01.275
8	Mike BRIGGS	1:01.088	8	James KAYE	1:01.291
9	Rickard RYDELL	1:01.095	9	Matt NEAL	1:01.450
10	James KAYE	1:01.232	10	Tim SUGDEN	1:01.456
11	Derek WARWICK	1:01.274	11	Mike BRIGGS	1:01.459
12	Gabriele TARQUINI	1:01.275	12	Gabriele TARQUINI	1:01.493
13	Simon HARRISON	1:01.280	13	Johnny CECOTTO	1:01.563
14	Tim SUGDEN	1:01.282	14	Rickard RYDELL	1:01.570
15	Matt NEAL	1:01.295	15	Simon HARRISON	1:01.758
16	Johnny CECOTTO	1:01.337	16	David BRABHAM	1:01.777
17	David BRABHAM	1:01.371	17	Tim HARVEY	1:01.782
18	Tim HARVEY	1:01.484	18	Patrick WATTS	1:01.837
19	Robb GRAVETT	1:01.914	19	Derek WARWICK	1:01.877
20	Nigel SMITH	1:02.031	20	Nigel SMITH	1:02.267
21	Hamish IRVINE	1:02.491	21	Charlie COX	1:02.370
22	Charlie COX	1:02.492	22	Robb GRAVETT	1:02.581
23	Richard KAYE	1:02.609	23	Richard KAYE	1:03.236
24	Patrick WATTS	2:51.270	24	Hamish IRVINE	1:03.745

RESULTS - ROUND 24
28 laps, 47.20 miles

			Time/laps	Best lap
1	Alain MENU	Renault Laguna	32:34.72	1:01.43
2	Will HOY	Renault Laguna	32:35.83	1:01.63
3	John CLELAND	Vauxhall Cavalier 16V	32:40.47	1:01.52
4	Kelvin BURT	Ford Mondeo Ghia	32:41.44	1:01.62
5	David LESLIE	Honda Accord	32:50.11	1:01.96
6	Mike BRIGGS	Vauxhall Cavalier 16V	32:51.37	1:02.10
7	Rickard RYDELL	Volvo 850 20V	32:54.44	1:02.20
8	Derek WARWICK	Alfa Romeo 155	32:56.15	1:02.43
9	David BRABHAM	BMW 318iS	32:59.20	1:02.31
10	Tim HARVEY	Volvo 850 20V	33:00.77	1:02.45

11 Patrick WATTS (Peugeot 405), 33:02.57; 12 Richard KAYE (Ford Mondeo Ghia), 33:23.67; 13 Tim SUGDEN (Toyota Carina E), 33:25.95; 14 Hamish IRVINE (Peugeot 405), 33:32.73; 15 Robb GRAVETT (Ford Mondeo Ghia), 33:33.95; 16 James KAYE (Honda Accord), 18 laps; 17 Matt NEAL (Ford Mondeo Ghia), 17 laps; 18 Paul RADISICH (Ford Mondeo Ghia), 16 laps; **Retired:** Charlie COX (Ford Mondeo Ghia), 24 laps, accident; Gabriele TARQUINI (Alfa Romeo 155), 24 laps, damage; Johnny CECOTTO (BMW 318iS), 22 laps, tyres; Julian BAILEY (Toyota Carina E), 16 laps, bodywork; Nigel SMITH (Vauxhall Cavalier 16v), 1 lap, accident; Simon HARRISON (Peugeot 405), 0 laps, accident.

RESULTS - ROUND 25
29 laps, 47.85 miles

			Time/laps	Best lap
1	Will HOY	Renault Laguna	31:55.43	1:01.34
2	Alain MENU	Renault Laguna	31:55.97	1:01.26
3	John CLELAND	Vauxhall Cavalier 16V	31:58.62	1:01.62
4	David LESLIE	Honda Accord	32:01.23	1:01.71
5	Julian BAILEY	Toyota Carina E	32:02.99	1:01.46
6	Tim SUGDEN	Toyota Carina E	32:13.48	1:01.87
7	Tim HARVEY	Volvo 850 20V	32:15.02	1:02.13
8	Patrick WATTS	Peugeot 405	32:15.64	1:02.47
9	James KAYE	Honda Accord	32:16.28	1:02.04
10	Derek WARWICK	Alfa Romeo 155	32:17.69	1:02.21

11 Matt NEAL (Ford Mondeo Ghia), 32:17.83; 12 Paul RADISICH (Ford Mondeo Ghia), 32:30.11; 13 Richard KAYE (Ford Mondeo Ghia), 32:30.32; 14 Charlie COX (Ford Mondeo Ghia), 32:51.04; 15 Gabriele TARQUINI (Alfa Romeo 155), 32:47.94; **Retired:** Robb GRAVETT (Ford Mondeo Ghia), 11 laps, accident; Mike BRIGGS (Vauxhall Cavalier 16V), 10 laps, accident; Johnny CECOTTO (BMW 318iS), 8 laps, accident; David BRABHAM (BMW 318iS), 3 laps, accident; Hamish IRVINE (Peugeot 405), 3 laps, engine; Rickard RYDELL (Volvo 850 20V), 2 laps, accident; Kelvin BURT (Ford Mondeo Ghia), 2 laps, accident.

FINAL CHAMPIONSHIP POSITIONS

DRIVERS

1	John CLELAND	348
2	Alain MENU	305
3	Rickard RYDELL	255
4	Will HOY	195
5	Tim HARVEY	176
6	Paul RADISICH	130
7	James THOMPSON	124
8	Kelvin BURT	117
9	Julian BAILEY	94
10	Patrick WATTS	61
=	David LESLIE	61
12	Johnny CECOTTO	49
13	David BRABHAM	48
=	Tim SUGDEN	48
15	Mike BRIGGS	35
16	Gabriele TARQUINI	33
17	Giampiero SIMONI	27
18	James KAYE	26
19	Derek WARWICK	15
20	Robb GRAVETT	13
21	Matthew NEAL	12
22	Simon HARRISON	9
23	Charlie COX	8
=	Richard KAYE	8
25	Jeff ALLAM	3

MANUFACTURERS

1	Renault	419
2	Vauxhall	414
3	Volvo	359
4	Ford	236
5	Toyota	172
6	BMW	144
7	Honda	136
8	Alfa Romeo	132
9	Peugeot	127

TEAMS

1	Vauxhall Sport	510
2	Williams Renault Dealer Racing	500
3	Volvo 850 Racing	431
4	Valvoline Team Mondeo	247
5	Team Toyota GB	142
6	BMW Motorsport Team	97
7	Honda Team MSD	87
8	Alfa Romeo Old Spice Racing	75
9	Total Team Peugeot	70
10	Team Dynamic	12

TOTAL CUP FOR PRIVATEERS

1	Matthew NEAL	430
2	Richard KAYE	342
3	Nigel SMITH	298
4	Hamish IRVINE	188
5	Robb GRAVETT	160
6	Charlie COX	110

AUSTRALIAN TOURING CAR CHAMPIONSHIP

FEBRUARY 5
SANDOWN-ROUND 1
1 Larry Perkins-Holden Commodore
2 Wayne Gardner-Holden Commodore
3 Peter Brock-Holden Commodore
4 Jim Richards-Holden Commodore
5 John Bowe-Ford Falcon
6 Tony Longhurst-Ford Falcon

1 John Bowe-Ford Falcon
2 Larry Perkins-Holden Commodore
3 Wayne Gardner-Holden Commodore
4 Dick Johnson-Ford Falcon
5 Neil Crompton-Holden Commodore
6 Tomas Mezera-Holden Commodore

FEBRUARY 26
SYMMONS PLAIN-ROUND 2
1 John Bowe-Ford Falcon
2 Tomas Mezera-Holden Commodore
3 Glenn Seton-Ford Falcon
4 Peter Brock-Holden Commodore
5 Alan Jones-Ford Falcon
6 Neil Crompton-Holden Commodore

1 Peter Brock-Holden Commodore
2 John Bowe-Ford Falcon
3 Tomas Mezera-Holden Commodore
4 Neil Crompton-Holden Commodore
5 Larry Perkins-Holden Commodore
6 Wayne Gardner-Holden Commodore

MARCH 12
BATHURST ROUND 3
1 Dick Johnson-Ford Falcon
2 John Bowe-Ford Falcon
3 Glenn Seton-Ford Falcon
4 Mark Skaife-Holden Commodore
5 Larry Perkins-Holden Commodore
6 Tomas Mezera-Holden Commodore

1 Mark Skaife-Holden Commodore
2 John Bowe-Ford Falcon
3 Larry Perkins-Holden Commodore
4 Tomas Mezera-Holden Commodore
5 Glenn Seton-Ford Falcon
6 Peter Brock-Holden Commodore

APRIL 9
PHILIP ISLAND-ROUND 4
1 Peter Brock-Holden Commodore
2 Alan Jones-Ford Falcon
3 Glenn Seton-Ford Falcon
4 Trevor Ashby-Holden Commodore
5 Tony Longhurst-Ford Falcon
6 John Bowe-Ford Falcon

1 Glenn Seton-Ford Falcon
2 Alan Jones-Ford Falcon
3 Peter Brock-Holden Commodore
4 John Bowe-Ford Falcon
5 Dick Johnson-Ford Falcon
6 Mark Skaife-Holden Commodore

APRIL 23
LAKESIDE-ROUND 5
1 John Bowe-Ford Falcon
2 Glenn Seton-Ford Falcon
3 Peter Brock-Holden Commodore
4 Dick Johnson-Ford Falcon
5 Tomas Mezera-Holden Commodore
6 Larry Perkins-Holden Commodore

1 Glenn Seton-Ford Falcon
2 Peter Brock-Holden Commodore
3 John Bowe-Ford Falcon
4 Larry Perkins-Holden Commodore
5 Tomas Mezera-Holden Commodore
6 Mark Skaife-Holden Commodore

MAY 21
WINTON-ROUND 6
1 John Bowe-Ford Falcon
2 Glenn Seton-Ford Falcon
3 Peter Brock-Holden Commodore
4 Neil Crompton-Holden Commodore
5 Alan Jones-Ford Falcon
6 Dick Johnson-Ford Falcon

1 John Bowe-Ford Falcon
2 Peter Brock-Holden Commodore
3 Glenn Seton-Ford Falcon
4 Tomas Mezera-Holden Commodore
5 Alan Jones-Ford Falcon
6 Larry Perkins-Holden Commodore

MAY 28
EASTERN CREEK-ROUND 7
1 Glenn Seton-Ford Falcon
2 Peter Brock-Holden Commodore
3 Mark Skaife-Holden Commodore
4 Alan Jones-Ford Falcon
5 Neil Crompton-Holden Commodore
6 John Bowe-Ford Falcon

1 Mark Skaife-Holden Commodore
2 Alan Jones-Ford Falcon
3 Peter Brock-Holden Commodore
4 John Bowe-Ford Falcon
5 Wayne Gardner-Holden Commodore
6 Neil Crompton-Holden Commodore

JULY 9
MALLALA-ROUND 8
1 Glenn Seton-Ford Falcon
2 Peter Brock-Holden Commodore
3 John Bowe-Ford Falcon
4 Dick Johnson-Ford Falcon
5 Tomas Mezera-Holden Commodore
6 Alan Jones-Ford Falcon

1 Glenn Seton-Ford Falcon
2 Peter Brock-Holden Commodore
3 John Bowe-Ford Falcon
4 Dick Johnson-Ford Falcon
5 Mark Skaife-Holden Commodore
6 Tomas Mezera-Holden Commodore

JULY 16
WANNEROO PARK-ROUND 9
1 Glenn Seton-Ford Falcon
2 Peter Brock-Holden Commodore
3 Larry Perkins-Holden Commodore
4 Tomas Mezera-Holden Commodore
5 John Bowe-Ford Falcon
6 Dick Johnson-Ford Falcon

1 Glenn Seton-Ford Falcon
2 Larry Perkins-Holden Commodore
3 Peter Brock-Holden Commodore
4 Mark Skaife-Holden Commodore
5 Jim Richards-Holden Commodore
6 Tomas Mezera-Holden Commodore

AUGUST 6
ORAN PARK-ROUND 10
1 John Bowe-Ford Falcon
2 Glenn Seton-Ford Falcon
3 Dick Johnson-Ford Falcon
4 Mark Skaife-Holden Commodore
5 Peter Brock-Holden Commodore
6 Tomas Mezera-Holden Commodore

1 John Bowe-Ford Falcon
2 Glenn Seton-Ford Falcon
3 Peter Brock-Holden Commodore
4 Alan Jones-Ford Falcon
5 Larry Perkins-Holden Commodore
6 Allan Grice-Ford Falcon

FINAL CHAMPIONSHIP POSITIONS
1 John Bowe-Ford Falcon
2 Glenn Seton-Ford Falcon
3 Peter Brock-Holden Commodore
4 Larry Perkins-Ford Falcon
5 Tomas Mezera-Holden Commodore
6 Mark Skaife-Holden Commorore

AUSTRALIAN SUPER TOURING CHAMPIONSHIP

MARCH 5
PHILLIP ISLAND-ROUND 1
1 Paul Morris-BMW 318i
2 Brad Jones-Audi 80
3 Greg Murphy-Audi 80
4 Tony Scott-Volvo 850
5 Steve Ellery-BMW 318i
6 Geoff Brabham-BMW 318i

1 Paul Morris-BMW 318i
2 Brad Jones-Audi 80
3 Geoff Brabham-BMW 318i
4 Tony Scott-Volvo 850
5 Justin Matthews-BMW M3
6 Mark Seymour-BMW M3

APRIL 2
ORAN PARK-ROUND 2
1 Greg Murphy-Audi 80
2 Geoff Brabham-BMW318i
3 Charlie O'Brian-BMW318i
4 Brad Jones-Audi 80
5 Paul Morris-BMW318i
6 Jeff Allam-Ford Mondeo

1 Geoff Brabham-BMW318i
2 Charlie O'Brian-BMW318i
3 Paul Morris-BMW318i
4 Brad Jones-Audi 80
5 Grag Murphy-Audi 80
6 Graham Moore-Opel Vectra

MAY 7
SYMMONS PLAIN-ROUND 3
1 Paul Morris-BMW 318i
2 Geoff Brabham-BMW 318i
3 Steve Ellery-BMW 318i
4 Graham Moore-Opel Vectra
5 Brad Jones-Audi 80
6 Mark Adderton-Peugeot 405Mi16

1 Geoff Brabham-BMW 318i
2 Paul Morris-BMW 318i
3 Greg Murphy-Audi 80
4 Steve Ellery-BMW 318i
5 Jeff Allam-Ford Mondeo
6 Brad Jones-Audi 80

MAY 13
CALDER PARK-ROUND 4
1 Geoff Brabham-BMW 318i
2 Paul Morris-BMW 318i
3 Jeff Allam-Ford Mondeo
4 Greg Murphy-Audi 80
5 Brad Jones-Audi 80
6 Steven Richards-Alfa Romeo 155

1 Paul Morris-BMW 318i
2 Geoff Brabham-BMW 318i
3 Jeff Allam-Ford Mondeo
4 Brad Jones-Audi 80
5 Greg Murphy-Audi 80
6 Tony Scott-Volvo 850

JUNE 4
MALLALA-ROUND 5
1 Geoff Brabham-BMW 318i
2 Brad Jones-Audi 80
3 Steve Ellery-BMW 318i
4 Greg Murphy-Audi 80
5 Paul Morris-BMW 318i
6 Graham Moore-Opel Vectra

1 Geoff Brabham-BMW 318i
2 Paul Morris-BMW 318i
3 Brad Jones-Audi 80
4 Greg Murphy-Audi 80
5 Graham Moore-Opel Vectra
6 Steve Ellery-BMW 318i

JULY 23
LAKESIDE-ROUND 6
1 Paul Morris-BMW 318i
2 Geoff Brabham-BMW 318i
3 Brad Jones-Audi 80
4 Steven Richards-Alfa Romeo 155

5 Greg Murphy-Audi 80
6 Steve Ellery-BMW 318i

1 Paul Morris-BMW 318i
2 Brad Jones-Audi 80
3 Greg Murphy-Audi 80
4 Steven Richards-Alfa Romeo 155
5 Graham Moore-Opel Vectra
6 Jeff Allam-Ford Mondeo

AUGUST 13
WINTON-ROUND 7
1 Paul Morris-BMW 318i
2 Brad Jones-Audi 80
3 Geoff Brabham-BMW 318i
4 Steve Ellery-BMW 318i
5 Geoff Full-Peugeot 405Mi16
6 Jeff Allam-Ford Mondeo

1 Brad Jones-Audi 80
2 Geoff Brabham-BMW 318i
3 Paul Morris-BMW 318i
4 Steven Richards-Alfa Romeo 155
5 Graham Moore-Opel Vectra
6 Jeff Allam-Ford Mondeo

AUGUST 27
EASTERN CREEK-ROUND 8
1 Brad Jones-Audi 80
2 Greg Murphy-Audi 80
3 Geoff Brabham-BMW 318i
4 Steven Richards-Alfa Romeo 155
5 Graham Moore-Opel Vectra
6 Steve Ellery-BMW 318i

1 Paul Morris-BMW 318i
2 Brad Jones-Audi 80
3 Tony Scott-Volvo 850
4 Paul Pickett-BMW 318i
5 Graham Moore-Opel Vectra
6 Steven Richards-Alfa Romeo 155

FINAL CHAMPIONSHIP POSITIONS
1 Paul Morris-BMW 318i
2 Geoff Brabham-BMW 318i
3 Brad Jones-Audi 80
4 Greg Murphy-Audi 80
5 Graham Moore-Opel Vectra
6 Steve Ellery-BMW 318i

DEUTSCHE TOURENWAGEN CUP

APRIL 30
ZOLDER(B)- ROUND 1
1 Frank Biela-Audi A4
2 Hans Stuck-Audi A4
3 Altfrid Heger-Audi A4

4 Tamara Vidali-Audi A4
5 Roberto Ravaglia-BMW 318i
6 Jo Winkelhock-BMW 318i

1 Frank Biela-Audi A4
2 Altfrid Heger-Audi A4
3 Roberto Ravaglia-BMW 318i
4 Peter Kox-BMW 318i
5 Jo Winkelhock-BMW 318i
6 Hans Stuck-Audi A4

MAY 14
SPA(B)-ROUND 2
1 Jo Winkelhock-BMW 318i
2 Hans Stuck-Audi A4
3 Jorg Muller-BMW 318i
4 Roberto Ravaglia-BMW 318i
5 Peter Kox-BMW 318i
6 Altfrid Heger-Audi A4

MAY 28
OSTERREICHRING(A)-ROUND 3
1 Frank Biela-Audi A4
2 Peter Kox-BMW 318i
3 Armin Hahne-Honda Accord
4 Roberto Ravaglia-BMW 318i
5 Alex Burgstaller-BMW 318i
6 Tamara Vidali-Audi A4

JUNE 11
HOCKENHEIM-ROUND 4
1 Frank Biela-Audi A4
2 Hans Stuck-Audi A4
3 Tamara Vidali-Audi A4
4 Altfrid Heger-Audi A4
5 Armin Hahne-Honda Accord
6 Peter Kox-BMW 318i

JULY 2
NURBURGRING-ROUND 5
1 Roland Asch-Ford Mondeo
2 Alex Burgstaller-BMW 318i
3 Frank Biela-Audi A4
4 Hans Stuck-Audi A4
5 Roberto Ravaglia-BMW 318i
6 Kieth Odor-Nissan Primera

1 Alex Burgstaller-BMW 318i
2 Roland Asch-Ford Mondeo
3 Frank Biela-Audi A4
4 Hans Stuck-Audi A4
5 Kieth Odor-Nissan Primera
6 Jo Winkelhock-BMW 318i

AUGUST 27
SALZBURGRING(A)-ROUND 6
1 Jo Winkelhock-BMW 318i
2 Peter Kox-BMW 318i
3 Roberto Ravaglia-BMW 318i
4 Klaus Niedzwiedz-Honda Accord
5 Armin Hahne-Honda Accord
6 Alex Burgstaller-BMW 318i

SEPTEMBER 10
AVUS-ROUND 7
1 Jo Winkelhock-BMW 318i
2 Peter Kox-BMW 318i
3 Alex Burgstaller-BMW 318i
4 Altfrid Heger-Audi A4
5 Hans Stuck-Audi A4
6 Roland Asch-Ford Mondeo

SEPTEMBER 24
NURBURGRING-ROUND 8
1 Emanuele Pirro-Audi A4
2 Jo Winkelhock-BMW 318i
3 Peter Kox-BMW 318i
4 Steve Soper-BMW 318i
5 Frank Biela-Audi A4
6 Hans Stuck-Audi A4

FINAL CHAMPIONSHIP POSITIONS
1 Jo Winkelhock-BMW 318i
2 Peter Kox-BMW 318i
3 Frank Biela-Audi A4
4 Hans Stuck-Audi A4
5 Altfrid Heger-Audi A4
6 Roberto Ravaglia-BMW 318i

DEUTSCHE TOURENWAGEN MEISTERSCHAFT

APRIL 23
HOCKENHEIM-ROUNDS 1&2
1 Bernd Schneider-Mercedes C Class
2 Jorg van Ommen-Mercedes C Class
3 Dario Franchitti-Mercedes C Class
4 Jan Magnussen-Mercedes C Class
5 Klaus Ludwig-Opel Calibra
6 Giancarlo Fisichella-Alfa Romeo 155V6

1 Bernd Schneider-Mercedes C Class
2 Jorg van Ommen-Mercedes C Class
3 Klaus Ludwig-Opel Calibra
4 JJ Lehto-Opel Calibra
5 Kurt Thiim-Mercedes C Class
6 Sandy Grau-Mercedes C Class

MAY 7
AVUS-ROUND 3
1 Kurt Thiim-Mercedes C Class
2 Sandy Grau-Mercedes C Class
3 Alessandro Nannini-Alfa Romeo 155V6
4 Giancarlo Fisichella-Alfa Romeo 155V6
5 Stefano Modena-Alfa Romeo 155V6
6 Michael Bartels-Alfa Romeo 155V6

ROUND 4 CANCELLED

JUNE 25
NORISRING-ROUNDS 5&6
1 Christian Danner-Alfa Romeo 155V6
2 Klaus Ludwig-Opel Calibra
3 Alessandro Nannini-Alfa Romeo 155V6
4 Bernd Schneider-Mercedes C Class
5 Stefano Modena-Alfa Romeo 155V6
6 Dario Franchitti-Mercedes C Class

1 Bernd Schneider-Mercedes C Class
2 Dario Franchitti-Mercedes C Class
3 Jorg van Ommen-Mercedes C Class
4 Stefano Modena-Alfa Romeo 155V6
5 Sandy Grau-Mercedes C Class
6 Christian Danner-Alfa Romeo 155V6

JULY 23
DIEPHOZ-ROUNDS 7&8
1 Michael Bartels-Alfa Romeo 155V6
2 Dario Franchitti-Mercedes C Class
3 Nicola Larini-Alfa Romeo 155V6
4 Alessandro Nannini-Alfa Romeo 155V6
5 Jorg van Ommen-Mercedes C Class
6 Giancarlo Fisichella-Alfa Romeo 155V6

1 Michael Bartels-Alfa Romeo 155V6
2 Nicola Larini-Alfa Romeo 155V6
3 Jorg van Ommen-Mercedes C Class
4 Dario Franchitti-Mercedes C Class
5 Jan Magnussen-Mercedes C Class
6 Bernd Schneider-Mercedes C Class

AUGUST 20
NURBURGRING-ROUNDS 9&10
1 Bernd Schneider-Mercedes C Class
2 Nicola Larini-Alfa Romeo 155V6
3 Sandy Grau-Mercedes C Class
4 Keke Rosberg-Opel Calibra
5 Jorg van Ommen-Mercedes C Class
6 Giancarlo Fisichella-Alfa Romeo 155V6

1 Bernd Schneider-Mercedes C Class
2 Sandy Grau-Mercedes C Class
3 Nicola Larini-Alfa Romeo 155V6
4 Kurt Thiim-Mercedes C Class
5 Ellen Lohr-Mercedes C Class
6 Jorg van Ommen-Mercedes C Class

SEPTEMBER 17
SINGEN-ROUNDS 11&12
1 Kurt Thiim-Mercedes C Class
2 Dario Franchitti-Mercedes C Class
3 Nicola Larini-Alfa Romeo 155V6
4 Jan Magnussen-Mercedes C Class
5 Manuel Reuter-Opel Calibra
6 Bernd Schneider-Mercedes C Class

1 Kurt Thiim-Mercedes C Class
2 Jan Magnussen-Mercedes C Class
3 Bernd Schneider-Mercedes C Class
4 Christian Danner-Alfa Romeo 155V6
5 Jorg van Ommen-Mercedes C Class
6 Yannick Dalmas-Opel Calibra

OCTOBER 15
HOCKENHEIM-ROUNDS 13&14
1 Klaus Ludwig-Opel Calibra
2 Manuel Reuter-Opel Calibra
3 Uwe Alzen-Mercedes C Class
4 Jorg van Ommen-Mercedes C Class
5 Alessandro Nannini-Alfa Romeo 155V6
6 JJ Lehto-Opel Calibra

1 Klaus Ludwig-Opel Calibra
2 Uwe Alzen-Mercedes C Class
3 Jorg van Ommen-Mercedes C Class
4 Manuel Reuter-Opel Calibra
5 Sandy Grau-Mercedes C Class
6 JJ Lehto-Opel Calibra

FINAL CHAMPIONSHIP POSITIONS
1 Bernd Schneider-Mercedes C Class
2 Jorg van Ommen-Mercedes C Class
3 Klaus Ludwig-Opel Calibra
4 Kurt Thiim-Mercedes C Class
5 Dario Franchitti-Mercedes C Class
6 Nicola Larini-Alfa Romeo 155V6

CHAMPIONNAT DE FRANCE SUPERTOURISM

APRIL 17
NOGARO-ROUNDS 1&2
1 Laurent Aiello-Peugeot 405Mi16
2 Alain Cudini-Opel Vectra
3 Philippe Gache-Alfa Romeo 155
4 Yvan Muller-BMW318i
5 Eric Helary-Opel Vectra
6 Philippe Alliot-Peugeot 405Mi16

1 Yvan Muller-BMW318i
2 Philippe Gache-Alfa Romeo 155
3 Alain Cudini-Opel Vectra
4 William David-Peugeot 405Mi16
5 Gerard Dillman-Opel Vectra
6 Jacques Laffite-Opel Vectra

MAY 21
DIJON-ROUNDS 3&4
1 Yvan Muller-BMW 318i
2 Eric Helary-Opel Vectra
3 Alain Cudini-Opel Vectra
4 Laurent Aiello-Peugeot 405Mi16
5 Philippe Alliot-Peugeot 405Mi16
6 Philippe Gache-Alfa Romeo 155

1 Yvan Muller-BMW 318i
2 Eric Helary-Opel Vectra
3 Philippe Gache-Alfa Romeo 155
4 Laurent Aiello-Peugeot 405Mi16
5 Alain Cudini-Opel Vectra
6 Philippe Alliot-Peugeot 405Mi16

JUNE 4
PAU-ROUNDS 5&6
1 Eric Helary-Opel Vectra
2 Yvan Muller-BMW 318i
3 Alain Cudini-Opel Vectra
4 Laurent Aiello-Peugeot 405Mi16
5 Philippe Alliot-Peugeot 405Mi16
6 Jacques Laffite-Opel Vectra

1 Eric Helary-Opel Vectra
2 Yvan Muller-BMW 318i
3 Jacques Lafite-Opel Vectra
4 William David-Peugeot 405Mi16
5 Alain Cudini-Opel Vectra
6 Marcel Tarres-BMW 318i

JUNE 11
CHARADE-ROUNDS 7&8
1 Eric Helary-Opel Vectra
2 Yvan Muller-BMW 318i
3 Alain Cudini-Opel vecrta
4 Philippe Gache-Alfa Romeo 155
5 Laurent Aiello-Peugeot 405Mi16
6 Jacques Laffite-Opel Vectra

1 Yvan Muller-BMW 318i
2 Eric Helary-Opel Vectra
3 Laurent Aiello-Peugeot 405Mi16
4 Alain Cudini-Opel Vectra
5 Philippe Alliot-Peugeot 405Mi16
6 Jacques Laffite-Opel Vectra

JUNE 25
VAL DE VIENNE-ROUNDS 9&10
1 Yvan Muller-BMW 318i
2 Laurent Aiello-Peugeot 405Mi16
3 Eric Helary-Opel Vectra
4 Alain Cudini-Opel Vectra
5 Jacques Laffite-Opel Vectra
6 Philippe Alliot-Peugeot 405Mi16

1 Yvan Muller-BMW 318i
2 Laurent Aiello-Peugeot 405Mi16
3 Eric Helary-Opel Vectra
4 Stephane Ortelli-BMW 318i
5 Philippe Alliot-Peugeot 405Mi16
6 Marcel Tarres-BMW 318i

JULY 6
CROIX-EN-TERNOIS-ROUNDS 11&12
1 Yvan Muller-BMW 318i
2 Eric Helary-Opel Vectra
3 Philippe Alliot-Peugeot 405Mi16
4 Stephane Ortelli-BMW 318i

5 Jacques Laffite-Opel Vectra
6 Alain Cudini-Opel Vectra

1 Eric Helary-Opel Vectra
2 Laurent Aiello-Peugeot 405Mi16
3 Jacques Laffite-Opel Vectra
4 Stephane Ortelli-BMW 318i
5 Philippe Alliot-Peugeot 405Mi16
6 William David-Peugeot 405Mi16

JULY 23
PAUL RICARD-ROUNDS 13&14
1 Yvan Muller-BMW 318i
2 Emanuele Naspetti-BMW 318i
3 Laurent Aiello-Peugeot 405Mi16
4 Eric Helary-Opel Vectra
5 Alain Cudini-Opel Vectra
6 William David-Peugeot 405Mi16

1 Yvan Muller-BMW 318i
2 Emanuele Naspetti-BMW 318i
3 Alain Cudini-Opel Vectra
4 Philippe Alliot-Peugeot 405Mi16
5 Eric Helary-Opel Vectra
6 Laurent Aiello-Peugeot 405Mi16

SEPTEMBER 3
ALBI-ROUNDS 15&16
1 Eric Helary-Opel Vectra
2 Jacques Laffite-Opel Vectra
3 Yvan Muller-BMW 318i
4 William David-Peugeot 405 Mi16
5 Stephane Ortelli-BMW 318i
6 Marcel Tarres-BMW 318i

1 Eric Helary-Opel Vectra
2 Jacques Laffite-Opel Vectra
3 Yvan Muller-BMW 318i
4 Laurent Aiello-Peugeot 405Mi16
5 Gerard Dillman-Opel Vectra
6 William David-Peugeot 405Mi16

OCTOBER 1
MONTLHERY-ROUNDS 17&18
1 Jacques Laffite-Opel Vectra
2 Eric Helary-Opel Vectra
3 Laurent Aiello-Peugeot 405Mi16
4 William David-Peugeot 405 Mi16
5 Yvan Muller-BMW 318i
6 Philippe Alliot-Peugeot 405Mi16

1 Eric Helary-Opel Vectra
2 Jacques Laffite-Opel Vectra
3 Laurent Aiello-Peugeot 405Mi16
4 Philippe Alliot-Peugeot 405 Mi16
5 Yvan Muller-BMW 318i
6 William David-Peugeot 405Mi16

FINAL CHAMPIONSHIP POSITIONS
1 Yvan Muller-BMW 318i
2 Eric Helary-Opel Vectra
3 Laurent Aiello-Peugeot 405Mi16
4 Jacques Laffite-Opel Vectra
5 Alain Cudini-Opel Vectra
6 Philippe Alliot-Peugeot 405Mi16

CAMPIONATO ITALIANO VELOCITA TURISMO

APRIL 23
MISANO-ROUNDS 1&2
1 Gabriele Tarquini-Alfa Romeo 155
2 Emanuele Pirro-Audi A4
3 Rinaldo Capello-Audi A4
4 Antonio Tamburini-Alfa Romeo 155
5 Emanuele Naspetti-BMW 318i
6 Roberto Colciago-Opel Vectra

1 Emanuele Pirro-Audi A4
2 Rinaldo Capello-Audi A4
3 Antonio Tamburini-Alfa Romeo 155
4 Emanuele Naspetti-BMW 318i
5 Fabrizio Giovanardi-Alfa Romeo 155
6 Gianni Morbidelli-BMW 318i

OCTOBER 8
VALLELUNGA-ROUNDS 19&20
1 Emanuele Pirro-Audi A4
2 Fabrizio Giovanardi-Alfa Romeo 155
3 Antonio Tamburini-Alfa Romeo 155
4 Rinaldo Capello-Audi A4
5 Will Hoy-Renault Laguna
6 Gianni Morbidelli-BMW 318i

1 Rinaldo Capello-Audi A4
2 Emanuele Pirro-Audi A4
3 Antonio Tamburini-Alfa Romeo 155
4 Will Hoy-Renault Laguna
5 Gianni Morbidelli-BMW 318i
6 Emanuele Naspetti-BMW 318i

FINAL CHAMPIONSHIP POSITIONS
1 Emanuele Pirro-Audi A4
2 Rinaldo Capelo-Audi A4
3 Fabrizio Giovanardi-Alfa Romeo 155
= Antonio Tamburini-Alfa Romeo 155
5 Gianni Morbidelli-Alfa Romeo 155
6 Emanuele Naspetti-BMW 318i

FIA INTERNATIONAL TOURING CAR SERIES

MAY 21
MUGELLO(I)-ROUNDS 1&2
1 Bernd Schneider-Mercedes C Class
2 Nicola Larini-Alfa Romeo 155V6
3 Jan Magnussen-Mercedes C Class
4 Dario Franchitti-Mercedes C Clas
5 Alessandro Nannini-Alfa Romeo 155V6
6 Stefano Modena-Alfa Romeo 155V6

1 Dario Franchitti-Mercedes C Class
2 Giancarlo Fisichella-Alfa Romeo 155V6
3 Bernd Schneider-Mercedes C Class
4 Kurt Thiim-Mercedes C Class
5 Nicola Larini-Alfa Romeo 155V6
6 Jan Magnussen-Mercedes C Class

JUNE 4
HELSINKI(SF)-ROUNDS 3&4
1 Christian Danner-Alfa Romeo 155V6
2 Stefano Modena-Alfa Romeo 155V6
3 JJ Lehto-Opel Calibra
4 Manuel Reuter-Opel Calibra
5 Bernd Schneider-Mercedes C Class
6 Gianni Giudici-Alfa Romeo 155V6

1 Nicola Larini-Alfa Romeo 155V6
2 Jan Magnussen-Mercedes C Class
3 Sandy Grau-Mercedes C ClAss
4 Uwe Alzen-Mercedes C Class
5 Ellen Lohr-Mercedes C Class
6 Kurt Thiim-Mercedes C Class

JULY 9
DONINGTON PARK(GB)-ROUNDS 5&6
1 Bernd Schneider-Mercedes C Class
2 Dario Franchitti-Mercedes C Class
3 Kurt Thiim-Mercedes C Class
4 Jorg van Ommen-Mercedes C Class
5 Giancarlo Fisichella-Alfa Romeo 155V6
6 Stefano Modena-Alfa Romeo 155V6

1 Bernd Schneider-Mercedes C Class
2 Dario Franchitti-Mercedes C Class
3 Jorg van Ommen-Mercedes C Class
4 Kurt Thiim-Mercedes C Class
5 Sandy Grau-Mercedes C Class
6 Manuel Reuter-Opel Calibra

AUGUST 6
ESTORIL(P)-ROUNDS 7&8
1 Bernd Schneider-Mercedes C Class
2 Jan Magnussen-Mercedes C Class
3 Nicola Larini-Alfa Romeo 155V6
4 Giancarlo Fisichella-Alfa Romeo 155V6
5 Dario Franchitti-Mercedes C Class
6 Kurt Thiim-Mercedes C Class

1 Jan Magnussen-Mercedes C Class
2 Bernd Schneider-Mercedes C Class
3 Dario Franchitti-Mercedes C Class

MAY 7
BINETTO-ROUNDS 3&4
1 Emanuele Pirro-Audi A4
2 Rinaldo Capello-Audi A4
3 Gabriele Tarquini-Alfa Romeo 155
4 Fabrizio Giovanardi-Alfa Romeo 155
5 Emanuele Naspetti-BMW 318i
6 Gianni Morbidelli-BMW 318i

1 Emanuele Pirro-Audi A4
2 Rinaldo Capello Audi A4
3 Gabriele Tarquini-Alfa Romeo 155
4 Fabrizio Giovanardi-Alfa Romeo 155
5 Emanuele Naspetti-BMW 318i
6 Antonio Tamburini-Alfa Romeo 155

MAY 21
MONZA-ROUNDS 5&6
1 Emanuele Pirro-Audi A4
2 Roberto Colciago-Opel Vectra
3 Antonio Tamburini-Alfa Romeo 155
4 Rinaldo Capello-Audi A4
5 Gianni Morbidelli-BMW 318i
6 Fabrizio Giovanardi-Alfa Romeo 155

1 Roberto Colciago-Opel Vectra
2 Emanuele Pirro-Audi A4
3 Rinaldo Capello-Audi A4
4 Gianni Morbidelli-BMW 318i
5 Antonio Tamburini-Alfa Romeo 155
6 Paolo delle Piane-Alfa Romeo 155

JUNE 4
IMOLA-ROUNDS 7&8
1 Emanuele Pirro-Audi A4
2 Rinaldo Capello-Audi A4
3 Gabrielle Tarquini-Alfa Romeo 155
4 Antonio Tamburini-Alfa Romeo 155
5 Fabrizio Giovanardi-Alfa Romeo 155
6 Emanuele Naspetti-BMW 318i

1 Emanuele Pirro-Audi A4
2 Rinaldo Capello-Audi A4
3 Gabriele Tarquini-Alfa Romeo 155
4 Antonio Tamburini-Alfa Romeo 155
5 Emanuele Naspetti-BMW 318i
6 Oscar Larrauri-Alfa Romeo 155

JUNE 18
MAGIONE-ROUNDS 9&10
1 Emanuele Pirro-Audi A4
2 Rinaldo Capello-Audi A4
3 Emanuele Naspetti-BMW 318i
4 Antonio Tamburini-Alfa Romeo 155
5 Gianni Morbidelli-BMW 318i
6 Fabrizio Giovanardi-Alfa Romeo 155

1 Rinaldo Capello-Audi A4
2 Emanuele Pirro-Audi A4
3 Emanuele Naspetti-BMW 318i
4 Gianni Morbidelli-BMW 318i
5 Antonio Tamburini-Alfa Romeo 155
6 Fabrizio Giovanardi-Alfa Romeo 155

JULY 9
MUGELLO-ROUNDS 11&12
1 Fabrizio Giovanardi-Alfa Romeo 155
2 Emanuele Naspetti-BMW 318i
3 Emanuele Pirro-Audi A4
4 Antonio Tamburini-Alfa Romeo 155
5 Gianni Morbidelli-BMW 318i
6 Oscar Larrauri-Alfa Romeo 155

1 Gabriele Tarquini-Alfa Romeo 155
2 Fabrizio Giovanardi-Alfa Romeo 155
3 Emanuele Naspetti-BMW 318i
4 Antonio Tamburini-Alfa Romeo 155
5 Emanuele Pirro-Audi A4
6 Rinaldo Capello-Audi A4

AUGUST 6
MISANO-ROUNDS 13&14
1 Emanuele Pirro-Audi A4
2 Rinaldo Capello-Audi A4
3 Gianni Morbidelli-BMW 318i
4 Emanuele Naspetti-BMW 318i
5 Fabrizio Giovanardi-Alfa Romeo 155
6 Antonio Tamburini-Alfa Romeo 155

1 Emanuele Pirro-Audi A4
2 Antonio Tamburini-Alfa Romeo 155
3 Rinaldo Capello-Audi A4
4 Yolander Surer-BMW 318i
5 Gherardo Cazzago-Alfa Romeo 155
6 Oscar Larrauri-Alfa Romeo 155

SEPTEMBER 3
ENNA-ROUNDS 15&16
1 Gianni Morbidelli-BMW 318i
2 Fabrizio Giovanardi-Alfa Romeo 155
3 Rinaldo Capello-Audi A4
4 Antonio Tamburini-Alfa Romeo 155
5 Emanuele Pirro-Audi A4
6 Moreno Soli-Alfa Romeo 155

1 Gianni Morbidelli-BMW 318i
2 Fabrizio Giovanardi-Alfa Romeo 155
3 Antonia Tamburini-Alfa Romeo 155
4 Emanuele Pirro-Audi A4
5 Rinaldo Capello-Audi A4
6 Yolander Surer-BMW 318i

SEPTEMBER 17
VARANO-ROUNDS 17&18
1 Rinaldo Capello-Audi A4
2 Emanuele Pirro-Audi A4
3 Fabrizio Giovanardi-Alfa Romeo 155
4 Mauro Trione-Peugeot 405Mi16
5 Yolander Surer-BMW 318i
6 Massimo Pigoli-Peugeot 405 Mi16

1 Emanuele Pirro-Audi A4
2 Fabrizio Giovanardi-Alfa Romeo 155
3 Rinaldo Capello-Audi A4
4 Gianni Morbidelli-BMW 318i
5 Emanuele Naspetti-BMW 318i
6 Antonio Tamburini-Alfa Romeo 155

4 Sandy Grau-Mercedes C Class
5 Stefano Modena-Alfa Romeo 155V6
6 Jorg van Ommen-Mercedes C Class

OCTOBER 8
MAGNY-COURS(F)-ROUNDS 9&10
1 Bernd Schneider-Mercedes C Class
2 Jan Magnussen-Mercedes C Class
3 Klaus Ludwig-Opel Calibra
4 Manuel Reuter-Opel Calibra
5 Stefano Modena-Alfa Romeo 155V6
6 Jorg van Ommen-Mercedes C Clas

1 Bernd Schneider-Mercedes C Class
2 Manuel Reuter-Opel Calibra
3 Jorg van Ommen-Mercedes C Class
4 Yannick Dalmas-Opel Calibra
5 JJ Lehto-Opel Calibra
6 Stefano Modena-Alfa Romeo 155V6

FINAL CHAMPIONSHIP POSITIONS
1 Bernd Schneider-Mercedes C Class
2 Jan Magnussen-Mercedes C Class
3 Dario Franchitti-Mercedes C Class
4 Nicola Larini-Alfa Romeo 155V6
5 Manuel Reuter-Opel Calibra
= Jorg van Ommen-Mercedes C Class

ALL JAPAN TOURING CAR CHAMPIONSHIP

MARCH 12
FUJI-ROUNDS 1&2
1 Tom Kristensen-Toyota EXiV
2 Anthony Reid-Opel Vectra
3 Masanori Sekiya-Toyota EXiV
4 Masami Kageyama-Toyota Corona
5 Mitsuhiro Kinoshita-BMW318
6 Kazuyoshi Hoshino-Nissan Primera

1 Tom Kristensen-Toyota EXiV
2 Masanori Sekiya-Toyota EXiV
3 Anthony Reid-Opel Vectra
4 Mitsuhiro Kinoshita-BMW318i
5 Steve Soper-BMW318i
6 Kazuyoshi Hoshino-Nissan Primera

MAY 14
SUGO-ROUNDS 3&4
1 Masanori Sekiya-Toyota EXiv
2 Michael Krumm-Toyota EXiV
3 Osamu Nakako-Honda Civic
4 Steve Soper-BMW 318i
5 Tom Krisensen-Toyota EXiV
6 Hidetoshi Mitsusada-Toyota EXiV

1 Masanori Sekiya-Toyota EXiV
2 Hidetoshi Mitsusada-Toyota EXiV
3 Osamu Nakako-Honda Civic
4 Steve Soper-BMW 318i
5 Satoshi Motoyama-Toyota EXiV
6 Kazuyoshi Hoshino-Nissan Primera

JUNE 11
TOKACHI-ROUNDS 5&6
1 Tom Kristensen-Toyota EXiV
2 Masanori Sekiya-Toyota Corona
3 Steve Soper-BMW 318i
4 Michael Krumm-Toyota EXiV
5 Akihiko Nakaya-BMW 318i
6 Masahiko Kinoshita-BMW 318i

1 Michael Krumm-Toyota EXiV
2 Hitoshi Mitsusada-Toyota Corona
3 Steve Soper-BMW 318i
4 Masanori Sekiya-Toyota EXiV
5 Akihiko Nakaya-BMW 318i
6 Toshio Suzuki-Nissan Primera

JULY 2
SUZUKA-ROUNDS 7&8
1 Anthony Reid-Opel Vectra
Steve Soper-BMW 318i
3 Kazuyoshi Hoshino-Nissan Primera
4 Hidetoshi Mitsusada-Toyota EXiV
5 Masanori Sekiya-Toyota EXiV
6 Akira Iida-Nissan Sunny

1 Steve Soper-BMW 318i
2 Kazuyoshi Hoshino-Nissan Primera
3 Anthony Reid-Opel Vectra
4 Masanori Sekiya-Toyota EXiV
5 Hidetoshi Mitsusada-Toyota EXiV
6 Michael Krumm-Toyota EXiV

JULY 23
MINE-ROUNDS 9&10
1 Akira Iida-Nissan Sunny
2 Naoki Hattori-Honda Civic
3 Tom Kristensen-Toyota EXiV
4 Akihiko Nakaya-BMW 318i
5 Takuya Kurosawa-Honda Civic
6 Hidetoshi Mitsusada-Toyota EXiV

1 Anthony Reid-Opel Vectra
2 Steve Soper-BMW 318i
3 Masanori Sekiya-Toyota EXiV
4 Tom Kristensen-Toyota EXiV
5 Jo Winkelhock-BMW 318i
6 Mitsuhiro Kinoshita-BMW 318i

AUGUST 6
TI CIRCUIT-ROUNDS 11&12
1 Masanori Sekiya-Toyota EXiV
2 Kazuyoshi Hoshino-Nissan Primera
3 Steve Soper-BMW 318i
4 Michael Krumm-Toyota EXiV
5 Anthony Reid-Opel Vectra
6 Akira Iida-Nissan Sunny

1 Anthony Reid-Opel Vectra
2 Kazuyoshi Hoshino-Nissan Primera
3 Masanori Sekiya-Toyota EXiV
4 Akira Iida-Nissan Sunny
5 Masami Kagayama-Toyota EXiV
6 Masahiro Hasemi-Nissan Primera

OCTOBER 8
SENDAI-ROUNDS 13&14
1 Jo Winkelhock-BMW 318i
2 Akira Iida-Nissan Sunny
3 Steve Soper-BMW 318i
4 Masanori Sekiya-Toyota EXiV
5 Justin Bell-Opel Vectra
6 Kazuyoshi Hoshino-Nissan Primera

1 Steve Soper-BMW 318i
2 Jo Winkelhock-BMW 318i
3 Akira Iida-Nissan Sunny
4 Justin Bell-Opel Vectra
5 Kazuyoshi Hoshino-Nissan Primera
6 Tom Kristensen-Toyota EXiV

NOVEMBER 5
FUJI-ROUNDS 15&16
1 Steve Soper-BMW 318i
2 Kazuyoshi Hoshino-Nisan Primera
3 Masahiro Hasemi-Nissan Primera
4 Masami Kageyama-Toyota EXiV
5 Hidetoshi Mitsusada-Toyota EXiV
6 Keiichi Tsuchida-Honda Civic

1 Kazuyoshi Hoshino-Nissan Primera
2 Steve Soper-BMW 318i
3 Masami Kageyama-Toyota EXiV
4 Tom Kristensen-Toyota EXiV
5 Masanori Sekiya-Toyota EXiV
6 Akira Iida-Nissan Sunny

FINAL CHAMPIONSHIP POSITIONS
1 Steve Soper-BMW 318i
2 Masanori Sekiya-Toyota EXiV
3 Kazuyoshi Hoshino-Nissan Primera
4 Anthony Reid-Opel Vectra
5 Tom Kristensen-Toyota EXiV
6 Akira Iida-Nissan Sunny

OTHER RACES

JULY 29/30
SPA 24 HOURS
1 Kox,Soper,Winkelhock-BMW 318i
2 Burgstaller,Duez,Piquet-BMW 318i
3 de Raddigues, Favre, Snyers-Honda Accord
4 Abt, Cremer, Haugg-Audi 80
5 Castagne,Hennes,Schoonbroodt-BMW M3
6 Hennes,Tant,Wagensetter-BMW M3

OCTOBER 1
BATHURST-Tooheys 1000
1 Perkins, Ingall-Holden Commodore
2 A Jones, Grice-Ford Falcon
3 Gardner, Crompton-Holden Commodore
4 Olofsson, Richards-Holden Commodore
5 B Jones, Percy-Holden Commodore
6 Scott, Cleland-Holden Commodore

OCTOBER 15
PAUL RICARD-FIA WORLD CUP
1 Frank Biela-Audi A4
2 Steve Soper-BMW 318i
3 Yvan Muller-BMW 318i
4 Johnny Cecotto-BMW 318i
5 Hans Stuck-Audi A4
6 Kelvin Burt-Ford Mondeo

1 Emanuele Pirro-Audi A4
2 Frank Biela-Audi A4
3 Steve Soper-BMW 318i
4 Yvan Muller-BMW 318i
5 Alain Menu-Renault Laguna
6 Johnny Cecotto-BMW 318i